Creativity in Flower Arrangement

Creativity in Flower Arrangement

Frances Bode

Photographs by William Bode

 Hearthside Press, Inc. **Publishers · New York**

Dedicated to our parents

Acknowledgements

It would be impossible to name everyone of the friends and members of the family who helped make this book possible, but I owe a special debt to William, who supplied husbandly advice, sympathetic photography, and constant support. My deepest gratitude goes to him.

To our children who survived an upset house and cold cuts; to my father, Theodore Maino, whose fine hand turned wood containers I cherish and enjoy; to my mother, who supplied rare and lovely materials from her beautiful garden; to Bernice Kinney, my loyal and true friend, always ready to help in any way; to Christine Davis, who shared her exotic orchids and gave me free access to her extensive vase collection; to Alma Coull, who shared with me the treasures discovered by a kindred spirit; to Iva Shepard, who has been friend, mentor and teacher; to George and Ed at Flowers Limited for untiring efforts to supply my needs in plant materials; to Marie Erwin, who gave me many lovely materials; to Humberto Montecan of the Tropicana Hotel, Puerto Vallarta, Mexico, who gave me cutting privileges; I acknowledge sincere and grateful appreciation.

A special thank you to Mrs. Nedda C. Anders, Editor of Hearthside Press, for her help and guidance; to Mrs. Kenneth Barrett, Flower Show School Chairman, and Mrs. William H. Barton, Revision Chairman for *The Handbook for Flower Shows*, National Council of State Garden Clubs, Inc., for their cooperation and good wishes; and to Emma Hodkinson Cyphers, whose contribution to today's flower arrangement cannot be measured, for permission to quote and for inspiration not directly acknowledged.

Table of Contents

Introduction

Is flower arrangement an art or a craft? This question presupposes a great distinction between the two words, yet to art savants the distinction, if it exists at all, is a narrow one. Consider, for example, that in museums like the Metropolitan Museum in New York, collections of furniture, metalwork, tapestries and porcelain exist side by side with canvases by Rembrandt and sculpture from ancient Greece. These crafted articles are valued as highly as the most costly paintings, not only by connoisseurs but by the general public as well. Where creativity is involved, therefore, it can be said that the words art and craft can be used interchangeably.

Some critics feel that flower arrangement cannot qualify as an art because it is ephemeral. Yet this makes as much sense as saying that dancing and singing cannot be so classified, for they too are ephemeral. However, recordings of the voice of Caruso and motion pictures of Nijinsky's dancing have preserved their great performances to be evaluated by posterity. Similarly, photographs can become an enduring record of the art of flower arrangement, making available for the judgment of the ages the artists' claims to creativity. Not only for this purpose, but for contemporary critics as well, I think that photog-

11

raphy techniques should be improved. There are too many head-on shots which treat floral designs as if they were two-dimensional. Instead, photographs should aim to picture the sculptural, three-dimensional quality of the work. It might even be useful to have arrangements photographed in a series of shots showing different views of the same design.

Why the new interest in creativity? The answer lies in the 1965 revision of the *Handbook for Flower Shows*, a publicaiton of the National Council of State Garden Clubs, Inc., which represents more than 15,000 garden clubs and 400,000 members. In this revision, for the first time a special Award for Creativity was announced. Nothing could more effectively have brought to the attention of the public (millions of whom annually attend flower shows held all over the country) the fact that from now on flower arrangement was to be treated as a creative art.

What is creativity? Why should it be a criterion for a special award? Why are arrangers interested in achieving recognition for creativity? Is it a will-o'-the-wisp thing that defies definition or evaluation? By no means! Creativity is that quality which elevates a flower arrangement to a work of art. It recognizes the existence of both the art and the craft of flower arrangement which are different but inseparable. The craft can be learned. This is the technical mastery required to accomplish the finished product, knowledge of both the possibilities and limitations of materials, mechanics and equipment. Good craftsmanship does not guarantee artistic excellence, however, for an arrangement might be technically competent in every detail yet be uninspired in either design or interpretation. Conversely, the most original and dramatic idea cannot be accomplished without the skill and knowledge of the craft. Art enters flower arrangement when there is a special spark that reaches out from the arrangement and strikes an answering response in the viewer or judge. It implies originality in design and in selection of materials, distinction in interpretation and intense involvement of the artist that is needed to communicate personal expression.

The Creativity Award poses a great responsibility for the judge. To be effective she should be knowledgeable about contemporary styles and forms of flower arrangement and conversant with current trends in this and other arts. As a judge, her decisions can influence the direction that flower arrangement will take. To be meaningful, the Creativity Award should challenge the arranger to new heights in design exploration and it is the duty of the judge to recognize and reward those who achieve these heights.

It is the purpose of this book to analyze creativity, how to achieve it, where to seek it and how to recognize it, not only for the flower arranger but also for the judge and the general public. A work of art cannot accomplish its ultimate purpose unless it *communicates* —and communication is impossible without sensitive, receptive and active participation of the viewer.

1

Creativity Begins with Craftsmanship

In all arts, there is a craft or technique which must be learned. We who choose to work with flowers must first learn how to support and control three-dimensional form, for it is useless to try to fit materials into a concept of beauty if they collapse as we work. Next, if the flowers, leaves and branches require it, as fresh ones usually do, we must find some way of supplying them with water. We must solve these two problems so gracefully and intelligently that whether we conceal or expose the mechanics which give support and water, the end result does not confront and alert the viewer to our strategy. An arrangement which carries the message "that big leaf at the bottom must be hiding the mechanics" or "what a clever contrivance for holding the stem" is badly designed. Good design is design which seems inevitable. Finally, we must be inventive in our approach to the usual materials of flower arrangement and alert to the possibilities of the unusual.

To learn the mechanics of any art is, as Havelock Ellis has said, an austere discipline, yet it is not without satisfaction. There is pleasure and excitement in discovering new techniques and new tools. In fact, there can be as much inventiveness, imagination and creativity in craft as there is in art. The pages which follow list some traditional tools and some contrived ones, and some old and new methods which I have found vital to creative design with mobiles, assemblages, collages and just plain flower arrangements.

Tools, Equipment and Techniques

Good work demands good and efficient tools and equipment, kept close at hand and in order. I have found a small, metal toolbox useful for transporting necessary equipment and a flat, rectangular basket tray most efficient on the work bench at home or for demonstrations.

Sharp shears and single-edged razor blade

Sturdy, strong, sharp shears, preferably with long narrow blades, are an absolute necessity for successful arranging. They cut cleanly without crushing the plant cells, thus allowing better water intake and extending the life of fresh materials. Slender blades make it easier to prune away unwanted flowers or decayed or too-dense foliage. Don't hesitate to eliminate excess material to clarify line and strengthen design. Raw cuts left after pruning can be made inconspicuous by rubbing them with ashes from the fireplace or ashtray.

A single-edged razor blade is useful for the many fibrous materials, yucca, New Zealand flax, etc., that are difficult to cut even with sharp

1.   Modern arrangers often use several kinds of mechanics in one design; only rarely exposing any of them. Here deeply grooved, pale green Armenian cucumbers and immature turban squash were impaled on chopsticks, then set in a pinholder without water. Heart-shaped philodendron leaves which repeat the dark green of the squash were kept fresh in a pin cup holding water. A medium green Japanese lacquer stand provides color transition to the pale green cucumbers. A satin-smooth dark purple eggplant adds color and texture contrast.

shears. Need leaves different from those in your garden? Use the razor blade to cut foliage down in size, following the natural shape, or restyle it as your design dictates. Slightly beaten egg white brushed along the cut edges is inconspicuous when dry, seals against moisture loss and will preserve trimmed materials for several days or through a flower show.

Needle-point holders (known as pin frogs in some regions) *and clay*

As a creative arranger, you have tremendous freedom to work with or without a background, make designs free-standing, suspended in space or backed against a wall. Instead of automatically placing the holder in the bottom of the container, experiment! For a new angle on flowers, fix the pinholder with floral clay to the *side* of the container or a small one on the *outside* to create the illusion of material growing through it. Because a needle-point holder should be concealed in the interest of neatness and good mechanics, it is well to use the smallest size possible that will still do the job. If the holder tips over with a heavy branch or one at an acute angle, try these techniques: Make a coil of floral clay to fit around the perimeter of the holder, position it and seal the edges smoothly against the holder and onto the container. Or, place three or four small balls of the new clay made expressly for styrofoam (Styroclay or Stickum) on the bottom of the holder before firmly pushing it into position. Both floral and styrofoam clay must be installed while the pinholder and container are thoroughly dry for they will not adhere if any moisture is present.

2. The oyster shell with its appealing translucence and purple-blushed white interior needs special control. If the base is thick enough, drill tiny holes close together, slip florist's wire through the holes and fasten to dowels. Poster paint touched on wire and dowels will hide them. Acanthus leaves and flowers radiate out in an intricate pattern which cuts up space.

A word of caution: styrofoam clay is difficult to remove but it can be dissolved by rubbing with a cotton ball saturated in cleaning fluid or salad oil (however, these can ruin some container finishes like bronze or wood).

Like all mechanical aids, pinholders have limitations. To expedite placing heavy, woody branches in a holder, cut them at a sharp angle; or split the end of the stem several times, place the branch straight down into the pins and gradually tilt it to the desired angle.

Do you have trouble making sweet peas, marguerites or grassy materials stay where you want them in a pinholder? For individual placements, wrap an inch or two of the bottom of the stem with strips of wax paper, newspaper, or aluminum foil before slipping them into the holder. A short length of calla lily, iris, cyperus, cattail or other pithy-stemmed material slipped over the thin stem will provide support and grip the pinholder. When you want a cluster of small flowers—violets, daisies, etc.—group them in your hand and secure with a rubber band, fine florist's wire or masking tape, before placing them in the holder. In all cases, however, be sure that the cut stem of the flower is exposed to absorb water.

The lead base of needle-point holders will tarnish and eventually corrode metals such as silver, brass, and copper if left for any length of time. Aluminum foil or several thicknesses of white paper napkin cut slightly larger than the holder will protect the container. On a perfectly flat surface, the moistened paper napkin also will prevent the pinholder from slipping or releasing so it is useful in containers other than just metal. A puddle of slightly cooled melted paraffin into which the holder can be set is an excellent way of securing it in either metal or glass. It can be jarred loose easily so you must work with care but it protects the metal and is inconspicuous in glass. Where you wish to completely conceal the mechanics in a glass container, a narrow strip of plumber's lead can be used as a sling to support the needle-holder just under the surface of the water.

Wire and tape

Florist's wire in various gauges is essential. Flowers with stems which are too short or slender can be wired to longer or thicker stems with 18 or 20 gauge. Fine green-coated 26- or 28-gauge wire is useful for grouping small-stemmed flowers or grasses, holding folded or manipulated leaves in the new shape or a flower in position in an arrangement. This type of mechanics *must* be concealed. A weak or hollow stem which does not stand upright can be firmed with wire inserted into it.

Scotch tape, staples, and pins are also useful in the flower arranger's kit. If a branch won't stay in place in a tall vase, you can make a grid of strips of Scotch tape across the top, but remember, Scotch tape will not stick to a wet surface or under water, so it must be above water level.

Floral tape, now available in a wide variety of colors, is useful for covering necessary wiring when extending or repairing stems, smoothing the contour and blending stems with the surrounding materials. Masking tape, strong and durable, is excellent for repairing broken stems or lengthening dry materials as its neutral color blends with that of the material. It also can be painted (Scotch tape resists paint) and will retain its adhesive qualities under water although it will not stick to a damp surface.

To make stems and stands

Wooden dowels, toothpicks, chopsticks, and natural stems and branches provide artificial stems for flowers, sea shells and other materials. To lengthen the stem of a flower, or to create a heavier stem for a fragile one, overlap it slightly by another stem and use wire or masking tape to hold the overlapped stems together. With fresh plant material, however, the cut end must still be long enough to reach water. Fruit and vegetables can be controlled by impaling them on inexpensive bamboo chopsticks from the Oriental grocery. Wooden

3.   (Opposite, left) Nature designed this sandstone sculpture but man made it a useful accessory for flower arranging. First a hole was drilled in the sandstone with a masonry drill, and a steel rod inserted. Then a hole was drilled in a pinholder and a brass tube, just a little larger in diameter than the steel rod, was soldered into the pinholder. The brass tube makes a socket for the sandstone sculpture on its steel rod.

Dried aloe flower stalks repeat the distinctive shape of the sandstone. An unusual bromeliad blossom casts intricate shadows on the stone, and a single philodendron leaf and cluster of palm bring color and form to this free-style design in a hand-turned modern walnut container.

4.   (Opposite, right) A permanent stand was made for this handsome piece of white branch coral. First, a one-quarter-inch dowel was secured in the center of a four-inch square of one-quarter-inch plywood. A hole was drilled in the stem of the coral with an electric drill, then the dowel was glued in it. Naturally-black fan coral skeletons, picked up on a beach in the West Indies after a hurricane, were wired to smaller dowels and wrapped with black floral tape, to make them inconspicuous. They could then be placed at any height and secured in a pinholder. Immature fan palm and staghorn fern leaves were placed in the smallest size of plastic orchid picks thus eliminating the need for filling the container with water, which would have ruined the coral.

dowels in varying sizes, depending upon the weight of the object being supported, make stems that can be installed on a pinholder. In Plate 12 the shells are just resting on lengths of ¼-inch dowel but in some instances the dowel is glued into a hole drilled in the object. Pairs of very small holes drilled in the oyster shells, Plate 2, made it possible to wire the shells to a dowel for support.

To make a stand for coral: Drill a hole in the center of a four-inch square of ¼-inch plywood. Set a ¼-inch dowel in the hole. Fix it in position with either white or Epoxy glue. Drill a ¼-inch hole in the stem of the coral with an electric drill and glue the dowel to the coral.

Supporting heavy rocks required a steel rod, which could not be put in a pinholder, instead of a dowel. My husband drilled a hole in the center of a needle-point holder and soldered into it a brass tube just larger than the rod, which holds it firmly. A masonry drill was used to make a hole in the stone, Plate 36.

Providing water in unusual places

Designing with flowers imposes certain restrictions on us—notably that we must supply them with a source of water. This is no problem in vases or other conventional containers, but can be awkward in drift-wood, shells, etc. Here are some mechanics to consider: *Plastic foam* (not styrofoam which is water resistant), soaked in water, can be shaped to fit any opening. To make it watertight, cover with house-hold plastic wrap, florist's foil or aluminum foil. *Sphagnum moss* can be used in the same way. Either one can be fitted into a crevice in a piece of wood or in a container that normally would not hold water. Glass or plastic orchid picks with watertight caps can be placed any-where, either concealed or deliberately exposed, depending on your need. Small water-filled *balloons* held on the stem with rubber bands or *fresh grapes* into which the stems are inserted make fresh flowers self-contained. They can then be placed wherever you want them in your design. *Sand* which can be moistened as necessary is useful for desert designs with cacti plants but it is not recommended for most fresh materials as it clogs the cut stems, preventing water absorption. However, dry sand is highly successful for supporting dried materials as it adds weight to the container as well as controlling the stems. It is valuable, also, as a partial filler for tall containers which would

5. (Opposite, left) Nylon tow rope, which has an unusual texture, is too limp for use, so heavy coat hanger wire was inserted in its hollow core, creating a rigid material which could be shaped into any line. Because water will penetrate alabaster container, the materials were set in a cup holder, masked with white aquamarine gravel. The gravel, echoing the tex-ture of the rope, serves as aesthetic as well as a practical purpose. Wood discs elevate the container and give visual weight.

6. (Right) A wedge of plastic foam made possible the use as a container of a white porcelain lamp base with an opening too small for a standard cup pinholder. The plastic foam, water-soaked, shaped to fit the opening, and covered with household plastic wrap, supplies water for the shell ginger flower stalk and philodendron leaves. You have to pierce the plastic with an ice pick to insert the stems and use care not to push clear through the bottom. The plastic seals tightly around the stems, preventing water seepage which would ruin the surface of the bases below.

otherwise require an inordinate amount of plastic foam. Fill the container two-thirds to three-quarters full of sand, and then pour a layer of melted paraffin to seal it. The paraffin provides a solid base for either a needle-point holder or a layer of plastic foam.

Combining dried and fresh material

If you consider dried flowers as expendable, you can use the same mechanics when you combine them with fresh as you would use for fresh flowers alone. But, if you have valuable or hard-to-replace dried things, you will want to protect them against the deterioration which comes when they are placed in water for any time. If the arrangement is mostly dry with a small amount of fresh material, place the latter in orchid picks or in a separate cup pinholder. In a predominantly fresh arrangement, you can preserve dry material as follows: dip the part that will be under water in melted paraffin, or seal it with four coats of clear varnish (simply dip stem into can of varnish, letting excess drip off before setting aside to dry). Some dried materials disintegrate, change shape or become odoriforous (dried kelp, for example) and these should be kept above water level on a chopstick or dowel "stem."

Making Mobiles and Designs with Moving Parts

A trip to the sporting goods store will provide you with several vital materials for constructing hanging or mobile designs. Nylon monofilament, used by fishermen for line and leaders, is a boon to creative designing. Barely discernible, it can be used in stabiles or mobiles or to make forms appear to float in space. It comes in various sizes, numbered by the pounds it will support. The primary or supporting line of a mobile might require 20-pound while the individual units may only need 2- or 5-pound strength. Of course, it is finer as the weight decreases so it is well to have a "wardrobe" of sizes to make the supporting members as invisible as possible in varied situations.

7. The stabile combines characteristics of both the mobile and the structure. This one is a study of form and movement in space. On a thick weathered plank from the California coast, a piece of creamy-white, alkaline-bleached, twisted wood was attached with screws. A beautiful, extremely hard wood form from the West Indies creates a cloudlike shape from which the mobile units are hung. Spiny sea urchins contribute an important form and texture contrast to the driftwood shapes. One devil's-claw suggests a bird soaring while another seems to be plummeting to earth. Two devil's-claws glued together add a strong form and needed visual weight in this constantly changing spatial design.

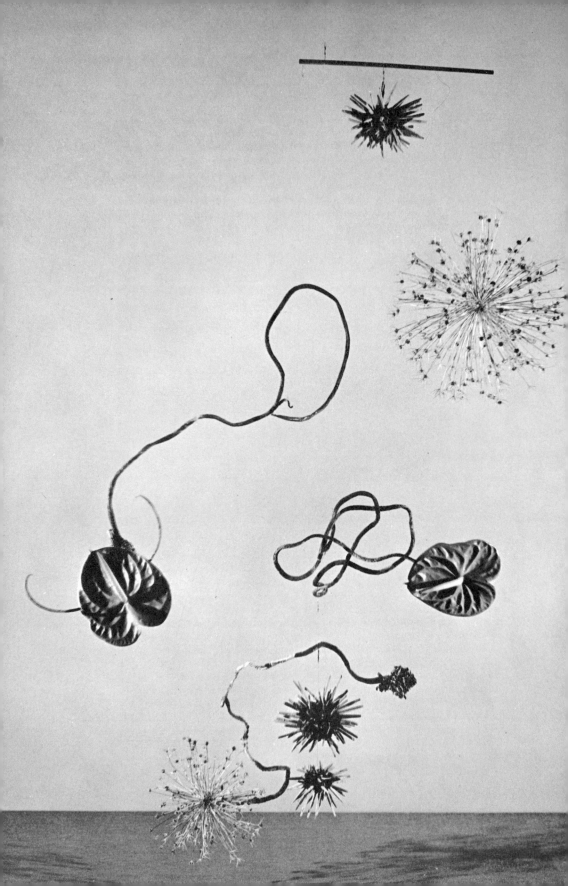

The tying of monofilament is foreign to arrangers although second nature to the sportsman. (Ask a friendly neighborhood sportsman to demonstrate.) A regular "granny" or square knot will not hold in this slippery material. First make an overhand tie and then, instead of a second overhand, pass the end through the loop of the knot three or four times before pulling it taut. This should be repeated at least two or more times before trusting it to hold. Pull hard on the knot to see that it holds firmly before proceeding.

Brass swivels, used by fishermen to make the lure free moving, do the same job in mobiles. There are two types of swivels and each is available in several sizes. One type has a spring catch on one end that can be used to attach the swivel to a screw eye; the other end has a ring to which the monofilament can be tied. A second type has two rings, used where movement is required in the monofilament between two objects.

Screw eyes, threaded loops of wire, are available at most hardware, hobby, or sporting goods stores, in many different sizes. To make them as inconspicuous as possible, the smallest practical size should be used, but often the threads are insufficient to hold in the material.

8. More than any other design, mobiles require an understanding of the mechanics which permit their units to move *freely* (not mechanically controlled) through space. Aim for variety in the shapes of the units. The juxtaposition of the shapes, the multiplicity of the movements, and the closeness of the arcs they describe as they move towards each other (make the paths as close as possible) are all factors contributing to the success of the mobile.

"Rendezvous," as this mobile is titled, was inspired by the Gemini space flights and was exhibited at the California State Fair Flower Show. As a flower-show piece, it required some fresh flowers, so small plastic water picks were glued on the dried kelp and wrapped in brown floral tape to hold water for the scarlet anthuriums. The units hang by almost invisible nylon monofilament with fishing swivels at the ends so that they can move freely, suspended from a bar which in turn hangs from the ceiling.

Screw the eye into position, remove, drop a bit of white glue into the hole and reposition. Let the glue dry at least 6 hours before putting any strain on it.

The mechanics of constructing a mobile so that all parts move freely in space with the actual weight properly distributed are tricky. I have found that it is easiest to start with the lowest placement and work upward to the primary supporting member, balancing each unit as it is added until the mobile is completed. Interaction of all parts can be tested as work progresses and fewer adjustments are needed in the last stages.

In a flower show, fresh material will usually be required. This can be incorporated by gluing plastic orchid picks to line material and covering them with floral tape. However, you must design with the water and flower in place for their weight will change the balance of the entire mobile if added later.

If you are planning to exhibit a mobile or stabile in a flower show, it should be made a week or two in advance to allow the monofilament time to stretch. One of the intriguing things about mobile or stabile designing is the "near misses" of the rotating forms but should the supporting members change length from the weight on them, the intended relationship could be changed or lost.

Creating Line Material

Never overlook any industrial material which has linear quality. The more eccentric the line, the better for your purpose because it will be refreshing to the eye. Nylon tow rope used by water skiers made possible the design in Plate 5. The tow rope is limp, so heavy coat hanger wire was inserted in its hollow core. The line could then be bent into any shape. Fine plastic tubing from a hospital supply store with a green-thread-wrapped wire inside replaces the brittle stems of minia-

9. Because today's designs are so strongly linear, creative arrangers are always searching for new patterns and shapes with which to work. A cable found along a roadside had twisted into this strange shape. To hold it upright, short lengths of Egyptian corn, also used to make the vertical line, were attached on each side of the cable with masking tape. The lengths could be set firmly in the pins of the cup pinholder (which was required to avoid damage to the wooden container). A rusted, sand-eroded chain covers the cup holder and contributes form and texture to this arrangement that features two Nightingale Fuji chrysanthemums.

10. A formation of jet planes making vapor trail patterns around a cloud inspired this free-style arrangement. The miniature cattails resembled the silhouette of planes but stiff stems limited their design possibilities so I created new stems with fine plastic tubing covering green, thread-wrapped steel florist's wire. The short-stemmed cattails were put in the end of the tubing, then the tubing was shaped in flight formation. A cluster of vanda orchids suggests the cloud which is elevated in space by the contrived container—an antique crystal lampshade permanently attached to a glass candlestick with Epoxy glue which dries clear and transparent. A rectangle of obscure building glass repeats the sheen of glass and plastic and adds contrasting linear pattern.

ture cattails to accomplish the design purpose in Plate 10. At holiday time, a glamorous arrangement could be made with velvet or metallic gold or silver tubing used in a similar way.

Discarded materials often have exciting linear possibilities if they can be exploited. I used a rusty speedometer cable in Plate 9, held erect in the pinholder by two short lengths of Egyptian corn stem bound securely to the cable with masking tape.

Driftwood Pointers

Actually, driftwood is a misnomer for wood is not only washed by water but also eroded or changed by the action of wind, sand or snow. Weathered wood appeals to the creative arranger. Wherever you go, mountain, lake, seashore, desert or river bank, be on the alert for interesting forms in weathered wood. There is an old adage among wood gatherers, "Kick it before you carry it!" If the wood is already disintegrating there is little value in taking it home but there are many treasures worthy of keeping.

Before you can use a new find in an arrangement it will probably require some treatment. If there is surface dirt and the wood is solid, wash it with a garden hose and forceful nozzle. In crevices, you may have to use a scrub brush or wire brush to remove stubborn or imbedded dirt. Always work in the direction of the grain to retain the natural surface of the piece. When there is fragile bark or delicate lichens that you want to preserve, wash more carefully, using a soft nylon vegetable brush or discarded toothbrush in hard-to-clean spots.

It may be necessary to trim away superfluous parts to reveal the true beauty of a fine piece. These can be sawed off, the cut chiseled and sanded to conform to the contour of the main line. If there is a color variation, shoe polish will blend the raw wood with the weathered surface. When a limb is cut from a piece of wood with bark or lichens, save the discarded piece and cover the cut with a piece of its bark or lichen, attached with white glue.

If you want to level a piece of wood, hold it in the exact position in which you want it to stand and lower the end to be cut into a bucket filled with water to the point where you plan to saw it off. This will give you a line that is absolutely level and an easy-to-follow guide for sawing.

When permanently combining several pieces of wood to create a new form or when attaching a base for support, wood screws and white glue are the best mechanics. Drill holes to prevent splitting the wood and put in a few drops of white glue before the wood screw is inserted. If the head of the screw will be exposed, countersink it below the surface of the wood and fill the hole with wood dough (a quick dry-

11.   Striated wood peeled from the root of a fallen juniper tree in the Sierras creates the structure for this arrangement. The bright orange and silver-gray lichens that contrast so beautifully with gray wood were revealed only after the wood had been washed and lightly brushed. The wood is wired (small holes were drilled for this purpose) to a dowel which was stuck on a pinholder in a Chinese pewter candlestick. Through natural openings in the root, fresh short-needled pine and stripped tips of new growth of another pine swing across in front of it. They are carried through, behind and up to the top of this massed-line design.

ing type of putty). This can be easily masked with a dab of matching shoe polish.

If you do not want to make a permanent structure, ¼-inch wooden dowels can be used as temporary pegs, inserted in holes drilled in both pieces of wood at point of contact.

A simple method for controlling wood or dry branches in a pin-holder is to use ¼-inch mesh hardware cloth. With tin snips, cut a strip two inches wide and twice the circumference of the branch. Leaving ½-inch of mesh extending beyond the end of the wood, wrap the hardware cloth tightly around the branch and secure with heavy florist's wire. The extended portion of this hardware cloth cylinder will hold securely in the needle-point holder. If the wood is to be painted (see *Painting and Spraying*, below), secure the hardware cloth in place before you begin to paint. This same technique can be used to hold candles or heavy large branches of fresh plant material in a pinholder. When you want to extend the wood outside the container, drill pairs of small holes and wire through to a dowel or chopstick which can be impaled in the holder.

Shell Pointers

Shells have been a design source and an inspiration to creativity throughout the long history of art and it is no wonder that today's flower arrangers are tireless beachcombers. The shells you find should be washed thoroughly with warm soapy water and a soft cloth, then

12.   These Philippine shells were covered with a calciferous layer which I removed to expose the lustrous surface underneath. To remove layers or skin, soak shells in a solution of muriatic acid diluted with water. Use a glass bowl and handle with extreme care—the acid can burn holes in metal, fabric and fingers! Wash shells in cold water, then in soapy water. Rinse throughly, dry and oil. Note: This will work on abalone, turbine, top shells and all which have a mother-of-pearl core, not with shells like conch which are calciferous throughout and would dissolve in acid.

rinsed in clear water. They will be more attractive if you soak them for a minute (or longer if you wish) in a solution of chlorine bleach diluted with water, then rinse again in clear water and dry. Oiling further enhances the brightness of the shells, so rub each one with baby oil.

Painting and Spraying

"A bit of spray and a bit of paint will make a flower seem what it ain't"—is ungrammatical but factual. In creative design for home use, there are no limits to your freedom to convert, color, distort or change the plants, cones, shells, containers, accessories and backgrounds which are to be used. (Warning—flower show exhibitors must follow the rules. See Chapter 6 and also *The Handbook for Flower Shows* or other official publications of the organization sponsoring the show.)

Sprays and paints

Florist's spray paints (Gard or Design Master), available at florist's supply and hobby stores, are my choice in most instances. They can be used with or without an undercoat on either fresh or dried plant materials, weathered wood, styrofoam and other plastics, as well as glass, ceramics and metal. They come in a wide variety of colors, many of them specifically related to or matching plant or flower colors—carnation red, moss green, jonquil yellow, Better Times, etc. Fast-drying light coats can be applied over each other as often as every five minutes.

Lacquer-based spray paints, available in many hardware, variety or department stores, are limited in use as they can only be applied to dry surfaces such as wood or dried or pressed flowers from which the drying process has extracted all moisture. They will melt styrofoam and sometimes destroy other types of plastic. In many types, too, there is a limited selection of color. One specialized paint, Rustoleum, now available in spray cans and in a variety of colors, is especially useful as it is formulated for use on metal, and retards rust inside the metal container.

Spraying techniques

Whatever type of spray paint you use, the directions given on the product should be followed, particularly about using several smooth, even, light coats rather than trying to cover in one thick coat, which will "weep" or run. The directions on all types of spray paints state that the spray can should be held from 10 to 14 inches from the object but this is one instance where experimentation can lead to some interesting and unusual effects. You can spray a container with a smooth coat of one color and overlay it with another color, sprayed at very close range to deliberately create runs for textural effects. To give only a hint of color to dried flowers, hold a spray can 6 feet above the objects to be painted. Spray for a few minutes, letting the color drift down and settle lightly. Cockscomb and hydrangea blossoms (pick them when they are pink, green or blue, and they will dry in their original colors) tend to become dull in the drying process but a drift of the original color—red-purple or greenish-gold—will enhance and brighten them without making them look "painted."

Florist's spray paints have a relatively soft surface which can be exploited. Several coats, each a different color, can be sprayed on a container or driftwood, allowing three to four hours drying time between each layer. When the final one has dried sufficiently, fine steel wool or a rag saturated in paint thinner or the two used interchangeably, can be rubbed over the surface, revealing the different layers as desired. I used this procedure on an antique iron urn, starting with chrome silver, then dark gray and finally, black. For raised areas, I rubbed down to the silver and left the black in the deepest indentations for shadow effects, the gray creating a middle ground.

Also, the inherent softness of this type of paint makes it possible to remove it easily from smooth surfaces which can add to the versatility of your container collection. The tall bottle in Plate 32 is normally white glazed porcelain but for this arrangement it was sprayed with several light coats of matte black. The only thing necessary to restore it to its original condition is to submerge it in warm water and detergent for an hour or so until the paint lifts of its own accord. Metal, completely glazed ceramic or glass containers can be used this way.

Caution: Do not use paint on wood or porous unglazed or partially glazed ceramic containers and expect to remove it by this method; it won't work!

Undercoating

Undercoating seals the surface of the material to be painted, expediting the process by requiring fewer coats to cover and a smaller amount of the final color. Driftwood, dried materials or unglazed ceramic can be sealed by spraying with several coats of clear acrylic-plastic or metallic spray paint. It may require three or four coats, applied over a period of several days (allowing at least twenty-four hours drying time between each coat) for a good base. Clear acrylic makes a good base for earth colors or black. If the final color of the material is to be in the cool range of greens, blues or white, an undercoat of chrome silver will give a luminous quality to the finished articles. For warm colors in the families of reds, oranges, yellows or browns, use an undercoat of gold.

You can get pretty, subtle effects, even in the undercoat, if you keep in mind the finished tones you want. For instance, one line offers a choice of several different golds including white, copper, brass, pewter and antique gold.

Antiquing

A new product available in the florist's spray paint by Gard, is called Antique Glaze which comes in ebony and walnut. It is designed to be used over painted surfaces or a Spra-tone Base Coat (same company) but in experimenting I found that it could be sprayed directly on untreated driftwood for interesting effects. The glaze dries very slowly so it can be sprayed over the entire surface, allowed to stand from 5 to 20 minutes depending upon the depth of color desired and then wiped off with a soft, absorbent cloth. It can be buffed almost entirely away on raised areas and left dark in crevices to heighten the shadow effect. On flat surfaces, you can create the effect of relief by leaving the middle areas lighter than the outer ones. (It will help you to visualize this if you realize that the effect of antiquing may have been caused by careless housekeeping! The theory is that the maids and ladies of the house wiped off the dust only by running a cloth in a rough circle around the middle of the object, leaving the dust to settle and darken the edges or sunken spots.)

There are many techniques for antiquing painted surfaces or for softening the effect on overly shiny glazed ceramic accessories and containers. There are several commercial products, some in kit form, and you should follow the directions for the specific product. A simple, easy method is to use artist's oil paints. Black, earth colors—raw or burnt umber, raw or burnt sienna, ochre, etc.—may be used depending upon the color of the undercoat and the final effect you want to achieve. With a soft brush completely cover the object with a thin layer of the oil paint, let stand at least a half hour and wipe away with a soft cloth using the same method as described above for highlights and shadows to enhance contour.

Blending, marbleizing and other effects

For a blended color effect, spray two colors at once from your spray cans. Using both hands, apply equal pressure on both cans, holding them at the same angle and the same distance from the object to be sprayed. For Christmas, many different metallic paints are effective in combinations: copper and bronze, gold and silver, color and a metallic, etc. Plate 33 shows material which was covered with two different values of turquoise, sprayed simultaneously over roots that were undercoated with chrome silver.

For marbleizing, apply two coats of a dark semigloss enamel. Let each coat dry for one day. Dampen a sponge with turpentine, dip it into a paint or metallic gilt that contrast with the base coat, and dab the sponge diagonally in rows across the object. A base of two coats of black with a contrast of white or silver paint is effective.

A quick and interesting effect can be applied to dried or glycerin-treated foliages—aspidistra, bird of paradise leaves, etc.—by spraying a metallic or color or combination of colors on the surface of the water in a bucket until there are blobs or "puddles" of color visible. Stir and spread the color with a stick and then quickly plunge the dried leaf in and out, through the scum of paint. Several leaves can be done before more paint has to be added. Each one will have an original and distinctive pattern. To be sure the leaf and paint are thoroughly dry, hang the stems with clothespins to a temporary line overnight before arranging with them.

2

A Creative Approach to Containers, Bases and Stands

Perhaps it would be best to begin this chapter with a definition. A container is something that contains or can contain something. It is not necessarily a vase, bowl, jar, or cache pot, although in traditional design it is likely to be. A container can be a tray, sea shell, leaf, or a piece of wood, and in modern flower arrangement it often is.

Antique Containers

Some curious superstitions have developed around the subject of containers. One of them seems to be that if a container is old, it has to be good. This is obviously ridiculous, because time will work no miracles on poor design. Therefore, two abiding rules for arrangers shopping around for antiques should be: *Don't buy it old if you wouldn't buy it new* and *Don't pay more for it old than you would if it were new.*

Collectors can protest that age *does* enhance value, and of course this is true from a monetary viewpoint. For example, carnival glass, tawdry stuff when it was made early in the century, is highly collectible today and relatively costly. But aesthetically, junk remains junk no matter how old it becomes.

13. This container, hand-crafted by ceramist Oyang explores several aspects of the natural qualities of clay. Its malleability is reflected in the irregular contour and the additional lower opening which adds to the container's usefulness for abstarct designing. The indented regular texture dramatizes the surface without destroying the form of the vase. Inspired by the curves initiated in the container shape, dead willow branches extend these into a swirling three-dimensional linear pattern. A single leaf and two Mauna Loa spathiphyllum blossoms occupy the shapes of space created by the lines and equate interest over the whole design area.

This is not to say that a container becomes *less* valuable or less useful with the passing of years. A vase inherited from mother, its gold rim slightly rubbed, or a silver bowl with dents showing the marks of use, have lost no shred of beauty or utility as they acquired the dignity of age. In fact, only the very young and immature—for instance the newly rich in an affluent society—put a premium on newness.

So apply common sense when you buy. Good design is ageless, but so is bad design.

Handcrafted, Commercial and Improvised Containers

Another fallacy of our time seems to be that anything is better if it is made by hand rather than by machine. There is a certain amount of truth here, but unfortunately not all amateurs designing clay, glass or metal containers are capable of producing good work. All too often we see examples of homemade containers which are exact replicas, complete with footed pedestal, of their commercial counterparts, except that the commercial ones have the advantage of having been properly fired (thus more enduring) and of being less costly.

Many contemporary ceramists are of course masters of the art of firing. Endlessly unique and inventive, whether carving intricate incised patterns or adding texture with overlays of clay, they exploit the malleability of their material without destroying its structure. If you are interested in buying handicrafts, take the trouble to visit local galleries, attend craft shows, and read books on the subject. These side excursions into other arts and crafts are making of flower arrangers the most knowledgeable group in the world!

Creative design does not exclude the use of a machine-produced container, provided it has good proportion, shape and texture. Another, and more important provision for using a commercial container is that it be a functional adjunct to the design, not a focus (as would be the case with a figurine used as an accessory—about this, see Chapter 3).

The container in itself, no matter how handsome, will not be the determinant factor in any assessment of the creativity or lack of creativity in an arrangement; all the elements of the design are parts of the total evaluation. But a badly designed container can totally destroy any possibilities of achieving a first-rate work.

Now let us consider the flower arranger who, while lacking interest in handcrafting, would still like to have containers which are original. These she can achieve by improvisation, combination and conversion, using objects which need not have been intended to hold plant material in their original state.

One such example is shown in Plate 10. For a free-style design, I wanted a simple glass shaft of a kind I have never seen commercially. Attaching an antique crystal lamp shade to a glass candlestick—homogenity of material and color is usually desirable in these combinations of objects—gave me just what I wanted. Epoxy glue was the bonding medium; being a resin glue it is waterproof and permanent for glass, clay, and metal.

Plate 17 illustrates another improvised container. A graceful abstract vase with a matte finish was too low for my needs. By gluing on a Japanese teacup with a similar glaze and tonal quality, I improved the proportion of the original vase and gave it needed height.

A container contrived of oddments of farm machinery—what an inspired idea this once was! I like to imagine a creative flower ar-

14. This commercial container would be a good addition to any container collection. Almost two feet tall, it has a simple graceful shape, a white stem and turquoise bowl. An added advantage is its frosted finish which is opaque enough to conceal mechanics and stems. Adaptable to many types of arrangement, it is used here in a free-style design of sago palm fronds and spathiphyllum leaves featuring a cluster of cattleya orchids.

15. Another good design for a basic container collection. A classic Japanese bronze usubata, with a patina which only age can produce, is a handsome container for hibiscus leaves which repeat the surface sheen of the bronze. The dead, lichen-encrusted branch of wild Catalina cherry echoes the reddish brown of the container. Brilliant pink hibiscus blossoms add strong form and a refreshing color contrast to balance the intricate pattern of the branch.

16.   A wisp of bamboo brushed onto a beige Japanese ceramic bottle inspired the design of this arrangement. A dense, shrubby plant, the bamboo was severely pruned to achieve a delicate pattern related to the simplicity of the painted design. In a simple statement of the essence of bamboo, the stems with measured, knobby joints, and the fingerlike pattern of leaves are clearly delineated in space. The lavender hybrid vanda orchids have a distinct speckled marking of brown that repeats the texture on the bottle.

17. (Opposite, left) Matchmaking can be fun! The straight-sided base with its etched design and the modern top with its double opening were quite dissimilar in size, shape, texture and line. But they have in common color (black) and material (clay), and so could be successfully paired. Epoxy glue joined them together.

They inspired the choice of plant materials: corkscrew willow and Mexican sago palm whose calligraphy echoed the design in the base, and small hybrid laelia orchids, closely related to the pattern of the top. This harmony of plants and materials containing them increases the bond between all the elements.

18. (Opposite, right) Nature is a superb designer of containers which can be yours for the finding. I saw this opened coconut on a beach in Mexico and combined it with a dramatic species anthurium which has a green and purple flower one foot long at the end of a curved stem. Purple taro leaves add weight.

ranger, living on a farm near a supply of abandoned equipment. Challenged to find a container for her flower arrangement, she saw in a plow disc just the shape she needed. Today it is hard to open a flower arranging book or calendar that does not have in it a reference to, and a picture of, a converted plow disc! I, too, have used it as you will see in Plate 62, but let us refer to the container only as a shallow round metal bowl!

It seems to me preferable to use simple commercial containers rather than to follow a path of *ersatz* originality. However, no matter how often repeated, designs from natural materials are never monotonous, because nature herself is never repetitive. In Puerto Vallarta, Mexico, where opened coconuts are used as cups for a drink known locally as Coco Loco, it was easy to see in them a natural bowl for flowers.

They Say "No Ornamentation"

No doubt rebelling against the overdecorated and sentimentalized legacies from the worst Victoriana, there has developed an aversion to any vase with painted, engraved or raised ornamentation. It is true that there were many monstrosities perpetrated on the public and that, even today, purposeless ornament can destroy the contour and form of basically good shapes. But decoration can also enrich an object, and be a source of inspiration. Although for a long time moderns were opposed to any "embroidery" on crafted objects, in architecture, and in interior design, I am glad to say that this trend has now been reversed. Even the most avant-garde designer has learned that stark simplicity is not the *only* validity in design.

Criteria for Container Selection

Whether a container is new or antique, mass-produced or hand-crafted, plain or ornamented, it should have pleasing proportions and good surface and color. Excessively shiny or overly ornate surfaces are generally to be avoided. They obliterate the basic structure, and they "take over," in the same way that cheap perfume seems to dominate over delicate and lovely scents wafting about in the same room.

This does not mean that all sheen is taboo. The patina of old metal, the luster of a well-done glaze on porcelain, the sparkle of clean crystal—these shine with intrinsic brilliance, handsomely reflecting the plant materials which they hold.

19. One never tires of using weathered wood, and it has a natural affinity for flowers. This dramatic locust stump found on a trip along the river was sawn to improve the proportion of trunk to branch, and to level it for stability. The color and texture interest of the pink aechmea and green miniature fan palm were distributed to equalize the linear force of the strong diagonal line and keep the eye moving over the whole abstract design. Moist sphagnum moss in deep indentations of the wood supply water for the leaves. Since there is space for other mechanics, the stems of *Aechmea fasciata* were wrapped in wet moss covered with household plastic wrap held by rubber bands. Then they were placed in the hole of the trunk and crotch of the limb. Both materials are naturally long lasting and, with water added regularly, stayed fresh for more than two weeks.

Texture, too, when it evolves from the actual construction, or is applied on the surface with meaning and force, without altering basic form, is always exciting. The hammer marks on the old French copper milk pail, the finger marks in the clay of a handcrafted ceramic container are legitimate; they are the signatures of those who crafted them.

Creativity Without Containers

The creative arranger evaluates every part of an arrangement in terms of its contribution to her intended design. If a container would destroy her plan, perhaps because it adds an unnecessary form, it must go. New techniques and mechanics no longer make mandatory the use of a container. Needle-point holders replaced conventional mechanics to allow more scope for individuality. However, since flower arrangements must rest on a solid surface, there are limits to one's ability to abandon all the traditional techniques. It is interesting to compare the abstract design in Plate 19 with the more conventional organization in Plate 20 in which it was necessary to mask a pinholder.

Bases and Stands

Is a base necessary? Traditionalists feel that it is a finishing touch, like a frame around a picture, defining the design area and elevating it from its surroundings. Those experimenting in the free styles are opposed because they feel that bases tend to put emphasis at the bottom of the arrangement, making them ground-oriented rather than space-oriented. The final decision made by the artist arranger must be with both design and function considered, but the ends must justify the means.

The base does have a practical function. It protects the furniture from the damage of water leak and from scratches caused by rough

20.   Using a completely different idea and design approach, this is a styl-
ized nature study rather than an abstract design as in Plate 19. The intent
was to dramatize the wood rather than subordinate it. The plant material
supported in a cup pinholder is used to give emphasis to the line and form
of the stump. Covering the cup holder required the use of the rock and
the pattern of crushed lava which, in turn, necessitated the use of a base
to unify the parts.

21. A footed stand is essential to the success of this arrangement, made in an antique bronze and marble urn. Without a stand the proportion would be chunky rather than graceful. The urn, although it would not be suitable for an extremely abstract arrangement, is compatible with traditional settings or with modern versions of conventional designs. Bird's-nest fern, palm and caladium leaves combine in a contemporary interpretation of an oval mass arrangement, with bold form, striking color and an open silhouette.

containers or accessories. Also a base is a safeguard when loose materials are used as a ground cover, with or without a container. A
base can serve as a defined horizontal plane, tying the components of
a composition, arrangement and accessories, into a unified whole, just
as a table top does. The base may be an important factor in visual balance, although it is never a crutch for crippled balance. Rather, it
should underscore carefully planned asymmetric design. The base
can add visual weight to a container, permitting the use of greater
height or heavier materials than would otherwise be possible.

Bases have gone through cycles both in use and in style. At first
only Oriental teakwood bases and stands were widely available, and
they were used regardless of style, materials or type of arrangement.
Then arrangers began using free-form bases, inevitably painted
black. The time has come for arrangers to take a long, hard look at
bases, whether to use them, when to use them and, most of all, how
to use them so they contribute to creativity.

Experiment with new materials and methods. Instead of those over-
used free-form bases, create them of crushed glass, rocks or gravel,
shaped to grow out of and integrate with the total design. Combine
glass, glass chips, wood, slate or gravel, for varied effects. Look to
architectural materials—crushed lava, sandstone or obscure glass—as
sources. Take a second look at the things around your home, trays,
fabric, mirrors, for they too have hidden possibilities. Experiment
not only with new bases, but with *no* bases. If omission of a base
would add more movement to a design—as it would if you were trying to give the effect of motion or wheeling—eliminate it. It may be
more creative and meaningful to leave out the base when it is not
needed as a design unit or to protect furniture.

22. A container is of wood, is of shell, is of clay, is of metal, and, if the arranger likes a challenge, is of glass. Glass, being transparent, requires special handling. To avoid interrupting the teardrop design inside this handblown Italian chartreuse glass vase, all stems were eliminated. A sling of plumber's lead was fitted into the top opening which supports a small pinholder just under the surface of the water. The lowest hosta leaf completely covers the mechanics, allowing the sparkle of the glass and its reflection in the mirror bases to become important elements. Sweeping curves of fresh Scotch broom fashion the linear pattern, punctuated by the strong form of red anthurium flowers and green hosta leaves. Note the completely different base used with the same container, opposite.

23. (Opposite) Using the same container as in Plate 22, the design was extended into the vase with a small staghorn fern leaf placed inside, upside down. More than a design element, it also covers the confusing stems of the other materials, repeats the shape of the primary vertical staghorn fern leaf, and points to the carefully organized shape of glass slag chips used as a base plane. A few drops of household bleach keep the water clear and retard growth of bacteria. Pairs of bromeliad leaves and nepenthes blossoms create a symmetrical motif around the solitary anthurium leaf.

3

Creativity with Organic Plant Materials

To the landscape architect, plants are not simply horticultural specimens but one of many materials used in designing a garden. A similar attitude must prevail for flower arrangers. For our purpose,
plants—and using this word I take it for granted that the reader will
extend its meaning to include such natural materials as rocks, shells
and wood—exist only for their design potential.

For example, consider English holly. The botanist knows it as *Ilex
aquifolium*, an evergreen of the family *Aquifoliaceae*. But the artist
sees a short-stalked, oval-shaped leaf about two inches long, strongly
patterned, with margins of large, triangular, spiny teeth and a dark
green, shiny surface reflecting broken light.

Or refer to Plate 24 which holds, according to Taylor's *Encyclopedia of Gardening*, the staghorn fern *Platycerium lemoinei*, some
members of the *Orchidaceae* family, and a few dead branches of a
fruit tree. Not to me, they're not. In staghorn fern I see a strongly
patterned, dynamic vertical structure ending in a deeply grooved
claw. It has a velvety yet light-reflecting surface. On a smaller scale,
seed heads and orchids repeat its form and pattern. The "dead
branches" are elevated horizontal lines which unify two parts of the
assemblage. All materials express strength.

24.   The design elements are staghorn fern leaves, parlor palm seed heads
and a cluster of orchids staged in ceramic columns, handmade by Ruth
Holland of Fair Oaks, Cal. Dead branches of almond lie across them in
an elevated horizontal that leads the eye to the hanging driftwood wall
pocket. A rusty wire, glued into holes drilled in the burned and water-
washed wood, creates interesting voids and links the two organizations.
Another link is the second cluster of orchids, placed in an orchid tube
painted to match the wood and glued inside the wall pocket. Deep-red
crushed lava from the garden shop unifies the assemblage.

Now it is true, of course, that many (perhaps the word should be most) flower arrangers grow their own plants but horticultural knowledge is not necessarily a concomitant of flower arranging. Indeed it is possible for one to become an expert floral artist using only florist materials, or wildlings from woods and roadside (if conservation laws allow them to be picked). But no one can arrange flowers in *designs* (as distinct from casual bouquets tucked into a vase) who has not understood the visual attributes of the plant materials.

Let the Plant Material Dictate the Design

In abstract arrangement the artist "takes what he thinks or feels is the essence of the material and attempts to communicate this to the observer" says the *Handbook for Flower Shows*. And this I think sums up the attributes of good designers in any medium—to find and express the fundamental nature of the material.

In the process of selecting materials for arrangement I have made some observations:

> Plants with gaunt, skeletal and gnarled patterns such as foliage of ailanthus, Scotch broom, pine, locust and small fan palms make strong features in a design. They show up well in space, or against large leathery leaves.

> Extreme shapes, like weeping branches or swirling heads of aloe, exert an immediate pull on the eye.

> Jagged or swordlike shapes of yucca and agave give strength to an arrangement. Rounded forms or cut leaves are a good foil for them.

> Densely textured evergreens like yew and spruce are good background plants. Boxwood, not as finely textured, is also good as a background.

Some plants—bird of paradise, caladium, philodendron—have as their chief asset an individuality of shape, color, or pattern. These can become pictures in themselves, like specimens in a garden.

Distinction in some plants arises only from the graceful poise of the flowers on their stems—billbergia, shell ginger, anthuriums. Such plants show up best if surrounded by space.

Why put dried flowers and driftwood, or any material which does not require water, into a vase?

Looking at misty seed heads of dandelion or salsify always brings me back to childhood days of lying on the grass for hours, watching the slowly moving clouds.

Conditioning Plant Material

Any foliage that is to be arranged, unless it comes from the florist, should be properly conditioned as it is cut, but conditioning is an *absolute necessity* for foliage which is to be trimmed and shaped. Here are the basic steps:

Completely submerge all hard or leathery surfaced foliage— such as aspidistra, holly, aralia, laurel—at least four to six hours or overnight.

Deciduous materials—purple plum, pistachio, hawthorne, crape myrtle, etc.—should be submerged in water from two to three hours and then placed in deep water to complete conditioning.

Velvety surfaced materials—geranium, mullein, etc.—or those with a flocklike surface—as dusty miller, platycerium—should only be under water one hour and then put into deep water for several hours.

25. Pine cone cores left by squirrels who had chewed away the petals
reminded me of the shapes which Calder used in his mobiles. They were
my inspiration for making a design with movable parts. The cones, suspended from silvery gray roots, are hung on nylon monofilament with
screw eyes in one end and tiny fish swivels in the other to give them mo-
bility. Columns of grayed blue-green desert artemisia repeat the shape and
color of the modern abstract Japanese ceramic.

26. The designer must understand her materials, and know what qualities they possess. Here warty mullein is used at its best as a strong, vertical accent, short-needled pine is placed to demonstrate its characteristically attractive pattern, and a diagonal of smooth wood which represents action thrusts itself forcefully into space.

27. Selective pruning of foliage from long-lasting fresh bamboo left an
almost bare stem which could be used at any angle, right side up or upside
down, as called for by the design. The few remaining sprigs of foliage add
a delicate tracery to the upright lines but required that their stems be
placed in water. Reminiscent of the garden appearance of the bamboo, a
tight cluster of foliage is used in one segment of this three-part, grayed-
green, modern Japanese vase. To prevent the leaves from curling and to
retain the fresh green color of bamboo, the cut ends should be placed in
very hot water and left until the water reaches room temperature. The
stems should be cut longer than required for the portion in the hot water
will discolor and have to be cut away.

Many woody-stemmed plants, notoriously poor keepers, bamboo, red barberry, peony, for example, can be conditioned by placing the stems in the hottest water from the tap and leaving then until the water cools. Warm water can be used to hasten the opening of iris or gladiolus that have tight buds. Snapping off the top two buds of gladiolus will also make them open faster in warm water. Cyperus, both papyrus and umbrella grass, lose their color very rapidly but if treated in hot water, will retain their natural green for several days. Any material conditioned in this manner should be cut considerably longer than needed in the arrangement as the hot water discolors the stem and this part should be discarded.

Some delicate foliage—calla lily, jack-in-the-pulpit, etc.—can be made to last longer by soaking it for from four to six hours in water to which the tobacco from a cigarette has been added.

Most flowers should be cut when the sun is off the plant, either morning or evening, placed in deep water (the entire stem, exposing only the flower itself) overnight in a cool, dark place out of drafts. The exceptions are the hollow-stem flowers, especially the narcissus family: they should be in deep water only one hour and then put into shallow water, three inches maximum, as the pressure of the water will collapse their stems. They should be arranged in shallow water also.

Foliage that is water-spotted or has surface dirt that does not come off when conditioned under water can be cleaned by adding a tablespoon of liquid detergent just before it is removed from the water, swishing it around and then placing it in deep containers to drip. If the water spots are stubborn there are several commercial house-plant cleaners that are available in spray cans which will remove the spots or a cotton ball saturated in milk rubbed over the surface will eliminate them.

For special occasions, Christmas or other holidays, you may want to lightly spray gold or other colors on fresh foliage. The conditioning methods above should be used, being sure that the foliage is completely dry and that the paint being used is one that is recommended for use on fresh plant material (florist's spray paints).

Photography poses certain problems for the arranger. It is *imperative* that all material be properly conditioned, as for a flower show. The floodlights used by the studio photographer emit tremendous heat which drains the vitality from plant material. However, the flash bulb or strobe, used by the news photographer or flower show visitor, is very rapid and there is little discernible heat. In this case, good conditioning will suffice, for there is not sufficient heat to effect the plant material to the same degree as under studio conditions.

Converting Natural Materials

The effect in planting may be natural, derived from the character of the plants used, or it may be artificial, based on making changes in materials as the French do in their lovely gardens. Similar possibilities exist for the creative flower arranger.

28. **Every garden has a clown! Some are created by accident, a bigger bush overpowering a smaller one and sending it off at a rakish angle. Some are in the nature of the plant itself, as in these bunching onions. Never content to grow just up, these individualistic materials develop a character of their own as they twist, turn and wrap around themselves and each other in fantastic shapes. Such materials, being easily bent or broken, dictate the design. In this arrangement, three stems of onion create a spiral in a black iron lotus-leaf Japanese vase. Two caladium flowers strengthen the vertical line of the central onion stem. A single caladium leaf echoes the wavy rim of the container and the rhythmic lines of the onions.**

29. Cleaning out the rosemary ground cover in the garden one day, I dis-covered this dying branch with just two ˙small tendrils clinging to life. These tendrils supplied detail interest and with a little pruning clarified the line created by nature. They became the dominant theme. A deep, wine-colored maranta bloom (rarely seen for it huddles in the tangle of leaves at the base of the plant) and maranta leaves make a strong form to balance the delicate, swirling line of rosemary. The two-level mottled blue-green ceramic Japanese well-bucket container is placed asymmetrically on the teak stand to emphasize the unequal weight distribution in the design.

Many leaves lend themselves to trimming. New Zealand flax, ara-lia, fatshedera, most palms, aspidistra, croton and sansevieria, may be trimmed and once trimmed, have excellent keeping qualities and good substance (if they are properly conditioned). To preserve the cut edges through a flower show see page 19.

Often within the structure of the plant lies a beautiful line or form that careful elimination of extraneous detail will reveal. Selec-tive pruning is sometimes necessary, as it was in the case of the diseased locust branch shown in Plate 31, to expose the dynamic design.

Weathered wood branches and roots are everywhere. Basic direc-tions for cleaning and preparing them are given in Chapter 1 when you want a natural finish. However, it may be that you want to change the color or wish to combine several disparate pieces to achieve a new effect. The wood can be painted (see Chapter 1) or bleached as follows:

> If the surface of a piece of wood is mottled or undistinguished, it may not fit the design purpose. The wood can be submerged in a solution of one part household bleach and one part water.

> It may take from one to several hours depending upon the amount of color you want to remove or the hardness of the wood.

30. One of the special treatments for dried materials involves dipping their ends in melted paraffin as a protective measure against decay. This was done to the stem of the dried desert weed which creates the primary structure curving upward. The second, inverted piece, swooping upside down, is supported by the lip of the container and required no special treatment. The fresh wisteria and golden brown cymbidiums stay fresh and are supported by water-soaked plastic foam in the brown Japanese modern container.

You should lift the wood out of the solution every half hour to check progress. If you notice stubborn areas, you can pour pure bleach on them, let it set ten to fifteen minutes, and return to the solution. When the desired color is attained wash thoroughly in several rinses and then soak for two to three hours in clear water. Allow the wood to dry slowly in the shade for it may split or crack in the sun. If you are combining woods in an arrangement or structure, you can bleach them to the same color or, if most of the pieces are gray in tone, the incompatible ones can be rubbed with a cloth dipped in wood ashes—this will give the unmatched pieces a similar gray surface.

It is possible to change not only the surface color but also the shape of many wood branches and roots. Soak the wood in warm water for several hours until it becomes pliable; it can then be shaped to the desired line. To hold it in position, wrap copper wire around it as copper does not rust and leave marks on the wood. It should be put in a dry, shady place until thoroughly dry before removing the wires.

Abstract Materials

Although modern flower arrangers seem to feel that they have discovered "abstraction," the world is full of it and always has been. A flower cut from a bush is an abstraction, because it is something separated from another thing. A form that is geometric rather than representational is an abstraction; a summary of the essence of something is an abstraction.

Why has creative flower arrangement come to lean so heavily on the technique of *abstracting*—of trimming, shaping, painting, distorting, converting, and otherwise removing from all natural context the materials of the art? The answer seems to me to be a simple one— a need to create not only the design, but the materials used in the

31. One angular contorted branch of diseased locust was pruned of extraneous lines and inserted upside down to establish the major space pattern in this modern ceramic with several openings designed by Sacramento artist John Landgraf. A second branch was placed in opposition and completes the space definition. A stem of shell ginger, stripped of all but one top leaf and an angel wing begonia leaf are interest points. They balance the knobby galls on the primary locust branch and keep the eye moving along and through the various areas of interest in this abstraction.

design. Finding shapes in nature is a passive occupation compared to that of bringing the shapes into being.

But abstraction should be purposeful. In Plate 61, the azalea was defoliated and clustered to concentrate its color, thereby giving it greater strength and bringing it into better relationship with the powerful roots.

Plant material and driftwood can be painted too (see directions in Chapter 1) provided there is a reason to do so other than the old army motto of "hammer to fit and paint to match." Do not assume that design errors can be corrected with paint, or that a traditional design can be made into a modern one thereby. In Plate 32, wood was painted matte black to match the container, and to create a strong structural pattern able to compete with the bold form and intense color of blossom and leaf. (I must mention that I would seriously consider the design relevance before painting anything black these days. Black paint has become the great cliché in abstract flower arrangement, so I would find another color whenever possible.)

In Plate 33, the turquoise porcelain design inside the stoneware bowl by internationally known ceramist Antonio Prieto of Oakland, California, inspired the arrangement and also the color which I painted the roots.

But unless painting makes a valid contribution to design and interpretation, it seems to me pointless because it destroys the vitality and texture of the organic form.

Drying and Preserving Plant Material

Drying can modify the color and texture of plant material, some-times changing the surface without altering the inherent design force or outstanding characteristics of the material. Agave blades become lighter in weight, more fibrous and coarse-textured as they dry but still retain their aspiring, triangular form and the swordlike character of the growing plant (Plate 34). To dry these required special treat-ment: after cutting they were placed in a covered cardboard box which allowed some air but little light to penetrate. It took two years to complete the drying process but they acquired a distinctive and colorful finish, not possible by natural weathering. There are basic rules for drying that I have found successful:

> Some materials must be gathered after maturing on the plant but before weathering changes the color or texture—mullein seed heads, cones, pods, palm boots or seed heads, New Zealand flax seed pods, etc.

> Materials that are very sturdy often acquire distinctive color or texture if allowed to weather on the plant before they are picked, such as the blossom stem of yucca or pulque.

> Most of the traditional dried flowers—strawflower, yarrow, sta-tice, celosia (plume and cockscomb), alliums in variety—should be picked at the moment just before maturity of the blossom, stripped of foliage and hung upside-down to dry in a dry dark place. As soon as they are thoroughly dry they should be packed loosely in covered boxes as light will fade the color.

> Common roadside dock, Egyptian corn, barley and many other grains can be gathered in various stages of maturity and color, stripped of leaves, bound in sheathes and hung to dry. You can have a collection of dock, for instance, in colors ranging from green through pink, rust and dark brown that will add interest and variety to fall or winter arrangements.

32.   This ordinary philodendron leaf turned a brilliant golden yellow and lasted for several days as the featured form in a free-style arrangement. The bold line of thick, weathered grape vine carves an aerial frame around the leaf. A thinner line rising out of the container carries the design into and through space. The circular patterns made by the stems are reiterated in the black container and bases.

Special treatment for dried materials

To preserve the fluffy heads of dandelion or salsify, or to prevent cat-tails from "exploding" you can spray them with hair spray. I have found that three or four light coats are more effective than one thick spraying which may cause them to disintegrate or give a "gluey" appearance.

Many common and popular arranging line materials, corkscrew willow, wisteria, Scotch broom, to name a few, can be shaped while still fresh, held in position by wrapping with copper wire (to prevent rust marks) and allowed to dry. If the material is particularly brittle, the copper wire should be cut with wire cutters every two inches to remove it rather than trying to unwrap it, which might break the branch. The foliage of South African silver tree *(Leucadendron)* in Plate 36 required special treatment. The fresh branches were wrapped with two-inch wide strips of old sheet to hold the leaves up-right against the stem. Over this copper wire was wrapped and the stem bent into the desired line. The cloth permitted the moisture to evaporate and when dry the wire and cloth were unwound revealing the distinctive texture of the material.

It is interesting to experiment with the possibilities of reshaping already dried materials. Many can be soaked in warm water until pliable, as the palm seed heads in Plate 43, wrapped with copper wire, shaped into the desired line and allowed to dry. When the ma-terial is heavy, as this was, it should be put in the sun or an airy, warm place, to prevent mildewing during the drying process.

33. A root that twisted, turned and spiraled in an ascending line was sprayed simultaneously with both pastel and brilliant turquoise paint to capture the varied color in the glaze which covered the porcelain interior of this handmade bowl. Bold shapes of bird-of-paradise leaves contribute weight and the flowers add exciting form and dynamic color contrast to the spiraling rhythms of this contemporary arrangement.

34. Three dried blades of agave or century plant, dried a lovely lavender, rose, gold and silver-gray and fresh green yucca leaves, repeating the
shape of the blades, are placed in a curved cup pinholder, tucked behind
the organization of dried pulque pods from Mexico. They provide interesting form and texture contrast to the other materials.

Treating materials with glycerin

Many different kinds of foliage can be given a new color dimension
and be made longer lasting if treated with glycerin. Only foliage that
is in good condition, without blemishes or insect damage, should be
used, for the end product is no better than that with which you start.
The basic process is to insert the stem of the branch into a solution of
two parts of water mixed with one part of glycerin. I have found that
the process can be expedited by using hot water and by splitting the
ends of the branch to increase its ability to absorb the mixture. *Do not
heat the mixture* but add the hot water to the cold glycerin. There is
no general rule about how long it will take for the length of the branch,
the kind of branch and the time of year will all affect the time required. When the material has changed color throughout, remove from
the solution, cover with a plastic cleaner's bag and hang where air but
not too much light can reach it. I have found that glycerin treated materials disintegrate very rapidly if stored in covered boxes.

The materials most commonly treated with glycerin are magnolia
and loquat but there is practically no end to the possibilities. I have
successfully treated several varieties of juniper, pine, pittosporum,
photinia, Oregon grape, aspidistra, laurel, aucuba, salal and many
others. I have found that different times of year will produce different
colors, as *Pittosporum Tobira* treated in the fall will be a soft honey
beige while that done in the spring will be a tawny brown. In the same
way "dollar" eucalyptus will vary from pale beige to grayed lavender (I placed the former in direct sun during the processing and the
latter in a dark corner of the garage). It is wise to keep making a

steady supply of glycerin treated materials for they get shabby with use and there is always the pleasure of trying something new and different in the "brew."

Storage Problems

The accumulation of dry and treated material that seems to be necessary now to do creative arranging is causing every arranger storage problems, not only physical space but also technical difficulties. I have found that hanging delicate and fragile line materials in small bundles from the garage rafters keeps them from tangling and breaking. Light fades or alters the color of dry materials which can be prevented if they are stored loosely in tightly covered boxes. Glycerin treated material will deteriorate if shut away from air although it, too, will fade in strong light. Plastic cleaner's bags make perfect storage since they are open at the bottom to permit air circulation but diffuse the light. They, too, can be hung from the rafters!

But the real problem in this tendency to acquire treasures is not storage methods or space but the threat to creativity. Unless you regularly and systematically sort through and eliminate you find yourself no longer stimulated by the materials. You learn to rely on them, using them over and over in the same way without re-examining their design potentials. Experiment with a piece of driftwood. See if it can be used in a different position or separated and reassembled into a new form. If it has no new possibilities, have the courage to dispose of it and make room for a new find that will inspire you to creativity.

4

Creativity in Choice of Accessories

The *Handbook for Flower Shows* defines *accessory* as "anything in the arrangement other than plant material, container, or background." At one time plant material meant only fresh flowers or foliage but today it is understood to include dry and treated plant material, as well as wood. In the light of this broader definition, then, *accessory* applies only to non-plant materials.

Natural Objects

Perhaps the reason that arrangers are intrigued with rocks, shells, coral and other natural accessories is that each one is a first, an original. As with plant materials, they too have been subjected to weather, heat, cold, erosion and change, which makes them unique.

The color and texture of natural accessories, then, may inspire the design and guide the arranger in her selection of plant material. Or, the shape of rock, coral or shell used as accessory may suggest design and materials. Because they are usually heavy and unwieldy, you may feel that natural objects limit creativity and must always be used in the same manner. But with appropriate mechanics, even heavy objects can be controlled (see Chapter 1). This means you can use them wherever you wish.

Between natural and man-made accessories are those natural objects altered by man. The Philippine shells in Plate 12 have had the calciferous outer layer removed with acid. The basic form remains but color and texture have been changed and refined. Although the fan coral in Plate 4 acquired its black skeletal form from the natural buffeting in a West Indian hurricane, the same effect can be achieved by placing natural fan coral in a pyrex dish and covering with pure household bleach. As soon as the outer yellow or lavender calcium layer dissolves remove the black skeleton from the bleach and wash thoroughly in clear water. Slag, the residue from glass factories, is a man-made material, but flooding with water when the slag pits are warm causes natural and extremely individual fracturing to occur.

Man-made Objects

Each natural object used as an accessory is an original but unfortunately man-made materials are usually mass-produced. This in itself is a deterrent to creativity. It is possible to use a new object out of context, like parts of machinery as accessories, but once done, this is no longer original.

Another way these man-made items can acquire individuality is from action of natural forces. The iron shackle and chain in Plate 37 were found in the ocean off Catalina Island. Salt water and sand created the color and texture that now makes this an original form, no longer identifiable as the machine-made components. The cork-net float, handle and Japanese glass fishnet float in Plate 35, although still recognizable, also have been acted upon by water, sand and sun, acquiring a highly individual texture and color. Commercial materials that can be shaped by the arranger or that take on a characteristic form from their original use, can be incorporated creatively in

35. Even mass-produced man-made materials take on individuality and character when exposed to action of the elements. Items that have weathered in the same manner seem to be most compatible. The action of desert sand and wind, for instance, is distinct from that of ocean salt water. The net-covered Japanese glass float ball, cork net float and knobby handle have a kinship with the unusual dried kelp, for all have come from the sea and have been acted upon by water, sun and sand. Suggestive of the plants beneath the sea, the grassy leaves and succulents bring fresh green color to this arrangement on a dark brown insulation cork base. The accessories add to the artistic effect, give weight where needed for balance, and help carry out the theme or spirit of the composition—thereby fulfilling all three requirements of the *Handbook for Flower Shows* concerning the use of accessories.

36.   A mottled rock whose surface resembled a serpent's skin inspired the choice of materials and design. A hole was bored in the rock with a masonry drill and a steel rod inserted to keep it stable in the hand-thrown ceramic by Sacramento potter Steve McGrew. Two dried branches of South African silver tree (the ends dipped in melted paraffin) establish the strong vertical pattern against the jade-green suedecloth panel. The green fruit on defoliated branches of Fried Egg Tree, so-called for its yellow-centered white flowers *(Oncoba spinosa)* trace a staccato pattern around the rock through to the horizontal plane of the Espresso brown base. The border of upholstery fabric repeats both the texture and color of the serpentine.

37. (Left) The iron form shown in this design acquired its basic structure from the chain it once was, but its present shape and texture is a result
of long immersion in the ocean. Brilliant orange and dark rust combined
with trapped sand particles give it an exciting color pattern. Subdued cool
tones in the other materials, silver gray driftwood, darker gray base and
grayed-green beach apple foliage *(Mesembryanthemum edule)* dramatize
the distinctive and warm color of the iron. A few loose links of rusted
chain on the left echo the color of the larger form and the shape of the
beach apple leaves. Thus the individual parts of a design inspired by the
original, nature-created accessory became a unified whole.

38. (Right) An old, solid pine duck decoy refinished in natural wood
color is used as an accessory in a hall-table arrangement. It helps "carry
out the theme or spirit" by its association with autumn activities, thus re-
inforcing the message brought by the warm color and harvest materials in
the arrangement. Mature Egyptian corn carries the busy texture and russet
color of the chrysanthemums through the whole vertical column. Intense
orange to red peppers contribute striking color; their smooth texture relates to that of the decoy. Dark green aralia leaves are a welcome cool contrast in this vertical massed-line study.

arrangements. The wire in Plate 63 was discarded by a crew repairing a chain-link fence where it had acquired this angular, wiggly line. Sprayed black and manipulated into the present shape it creates a vital, interesting line pattern which could be achieved with no other material. Under such conditions—that is, where man-made materials are made distinctive—I feel that their use is valid, reflecting the products of our machine-conscious age. It is justifiable, too, when the particular qualities of a man-made material are an important contribution to a design solution, as the color and light effects of glass in Plates 57 and 64. However, when machine-made material is incorporated at the expense of plant material which might have been used, for no better reason than to be different, it is nothing more than a gimmick.

Figurines

So far I have referred only to nonrepresentational man-made materials but what about the reproductions of figurines and sculpture which abound in the stores, and which we see advertised in magazines each month? Here, I think, the answer is clear cut: in my opinion no commercial figurine or statue should ever be used in an arrangement which is meant to reach the level of art. I believe that no arrangement with such an accessory should be considered for the Creativity Award at flower shows. My reasoning is as follows: Figurines are humanizers in a design; they relate the world of plants to the world of man. Because of this, they are *always* an absolute focus in a design. They pull the eye. Anything of such pre-eminence, I believe, must be unique and original. There are many statues of St. Francis, many mass-produced Madonnas, which I have seen too often to ever look upon again with a fresh eye. I have seen many nice little designs including them, but art must be imaginative, fresh, and original; it must be more than just pretty.

This restriction on the use of mass-produced figurines should not be imposed on containers, in my opinion. Containers are functional forms that can be integrated into any design plan; all that is required of them is that they have good design.

Antique Accessories—Objets d'Art

Original sculpture is too costly to be acquired by most of us, but this does not mean that all representational objects are excluded. Search in second-hand and antique shops can be rewarding, for there are many handcrafted objects from an earlier day. For traditional designs (and creativity is not limited only to modern work either by National Council rules for the Creativity Award or in general practice) you can find old porcelain figures and other designs that can inspire original design approaches. Although many antique figurines were not "one of a kind" originally, time, breakage and loss have now given them a singular position. Too, in past ages, although the body of the figurine was produced in molds, the final finishing, either with paint or glaze, was hand done, exhibiting both the taste and skill of the artisan. In this way each finished article was essentially an original.

Some representational objects that were mass-produced for functional purposes, like iron hitching posts, have acquired a unique patina from action of natural forces. Functional handcrafted objects like the pine decoy in Plate 38 can be given a new usefulness by refinishing. Stripped of its original paint and waxed to a fine luster it makes a beautiful accessory.

Handmade art objects like the iron and brass praying mantis in Plate 39 are not expensive and they are fun to find and use. Look for individuality and silhouette interest when you buy any original figurine whether it is a native, peasant handcraft or modern artist's work.

39. An amusing hand-crafted praying mantis has been an inspiration for many design interpretations. Made of black iron with brass wings, it has varied and interesting lines, one of which suggested this free-style arrangement. The nerine lily suggestive of the antennae and the corkscrew willow suggestive of a wirelike frame of the insect accessory were immediate choices for plant material, reinforced by gay red lilies and bright red and green caladium leaves.

40. (Opposite) Using an accessory which is factually related to the main body of the design, in this case the container, is the simplest means of achieving unity. The Chinese incense burner, the pattern on its lid, the teakwood stand, bear an obvious design relationship to each other but they also have elements of contrast, notably of size and form.

41.   Designed in the current idiom of "Pop" art, this composition is en-
titled "Picnic in the Park." Thinking of a park as a broad vista, I used an
open frame to define the height and width while allowing unlimited
depth. The park is suggested by the free-form grass area and Oregon grape
"tree" and picnic by crumpled paper napkins, picnic baskets, soda pop,
oranges, and bugs. Day lilies foreshadow the time to pick up and head for
home. There is a pervading sense of fun, a tongue-in-cheek approach, when
converting one type of art into another medium. It may be a fleeting
statement but the principles of design apply in this assemblage as in any
other flower arrangement.

Accessories and the Assemblage

Although the assemblage (see Chapter 7) has been identified as a special form of flower arrangement only since the publication of the 1965 revision of the *Handbook for Flower Shows*, it is actually an extension of a practice most familiar to our grandmothers! As a small child I remember with delight going to my great-aunt's house and, if I was very good, being allowed to listen to the ocean roaring in a giant sea shell from her parlor whatnot shelf. That shelf held a world of fascination to me with objects and treasures from a lifetime of collecting. Alas, with the introduction of the stark "moderne" interior design of the Twenties, these bibelots were banished as "clutter" and only one or two decorative items were permitted to be shown. Simplicity became a status symbol and the shells, figurines, ornamental vases and family photographs disappeared from the scene. Like all actions, this too had an equal and opposite reaction! Today we are seeing the return of decorative items in interior decoration, but with a difference. No longer grouped in an isolated whatnot shelf or on the top of a piano, personal treasures are part of the interior designer's tools. Interesting groupings of pictures or collections hung on the wall create a background for a table or desk that holds a flower arrangement and related accessories—candles, figurines, shells—in other words, an assemblage. The unifying factor may be color, texture, period or theme.

In the art of flower arrangement the extension of this idea of assembling compatible parts into an "assemblage" differs only in that the artist has greater freedom in selection of all parts since the wall color, furniture style or drapery pattern is not fixed. The arranger assembles flowers, dry materials and accessories, organizing them in a design against a background or in a niche to interpret a theme, project an idea or an emotion. The accessory (one or several) is chosen as it relates to the arranger's intent and is not necessarily used in its origi-

42.   A handsome stone carving from Mexico has a primitive force and bold silhouette, and a pattern and materials of equal strength were indicated. The intense color and distinct form of the Lobster Claw heliconia establish vertical planes in front of and behind the figure. Bromeliad blossoms repeat the color of the heliconia and the texture of the water-washed beach stones in the slate bases. There is a pleasing correlation between the vertical lines incised on the figure, the heliconia stems, and the edges of the dark red panel in the background of this assemblage.

nal context. A glass float ball may be used as a bubble in an assemblage suggesting an underwater mood. Starfish from the sea could be used to depict celestial stars in an interpretation of "night skies."

The selection of an accessory for an assemblage is made with a totally different point of view from that when the accessory is to be part of or accompanying an arrangement. In the assemblage, the accessory may inspire the whole interpretation rather than be subservient to both design and plant material. Representational objects can establish the theme, reinforce an idea or suggest a mood, with all plant material, natural accessories and background contributing to the total effect. In Plate 42 the stone figurine from Mexico is a symbol of strength and virility, bold in form and design. The selection of heliconia, bromeliad blossoms, slate and pebbles was determined by the figure. Although the various elements are disparate in origin (Mexico, Hawaii and California), their inherent compatibility as to form, color and texture creates a unified picture.

Accessories Reinforce a Mood or Spirit

Accessories alone cannot bear the burden of projecting an idea, theme or mood, but they can help to establish it. In interpretive arranging, the artist must know her subject and be conversant with the subtle as well as the obvious symbols related to it. It is impossible to react to,

43.   Putting the emphasis on the arrangement rather than the print, as in color plate opposite, this illustrates the intent when a schedule asks for a composition *inspired by* a picture. The print seems to have become smaller but this, of course, is because the arrangement is larger—the proportions have changed. Using the wave theme of the print, it is translated into the rhythmic curves of dried palm seed stalks and fresh aspidistra. Waving incised lines on the handmade container by Ruth Holland repeat the motif. Orange cathedral glass and turquoise glass slag chips create a pattern on the horizontal plane, relating the arrangement by direction and color to the print.

I. When a flower-show schedule requires an arrangement to *complement* a picture, the intent is for the picture to dominate the composition and the arrangement to be in scale with it. This abstract hand-screened print by Woods/Osborn of Nevada City, California, is titled "The Elements: Water." In an unusual white Japanese abstract container, Washington palm curls and fresh green clivia leaves reiterate the breaking wave motif of the print in mood, tempo and form. A single orange sisal "flower" picks up the flickering highlights of orange in the picture. Although both the print and the arrangement are self-contained and could stand alone, they each gain in meaning and impact as a composition.

II. (Left) "Still Life with Dice" by Juan Gris inspired this ensemble. The Cubists, early abstractionists, would take an object apart and reassemble it, but with some element of difference. For example, a wine glass kept its recognizable shape, but was rendered in wood. Two aspects were often presented simultaneously, perhaps a head-on and profile view. And Cubists achieved dimension by using strong contrast of hue and value. So in my assemblage I translated the spirit rather than the body of the Gris painting. Dried garlic heads and a square container were abstracts of dice. Fabrics and leaves in contrasting values pinned on the background and base created a sense of depth.

III. (Right) The Cubist theme of extracting elements from an object and reassembling them in an abstract way inspired this wall plaque of fruits and vegetables, whole, split and sliced, fastened with toothpicks and pins on red and white plain vinyl. Impermanent and perishable, it serves no purpose other than as a design experiment but it could be used for a flower show if cut surfaces were sealed with slightly beaten egg white.

IV. (Opposite, above) This design featuring curves was designed around Cup of Gold *(Solandra guttata)* and its handsomely poised blossoms. First the bud swells until it is seven or eight inches long, gradually turning from green to chartreuse. In a few days it opens into an exquisite clear yellow chalice with subtle brownish-purple stripes and crisp, erect stamen.

V. The base serves an aesthetic and practical function in this modern mass arrangement, unifying lid, container and plants, adding visual weight to balance the intricate pattern of the design, and finally, protecting the table top! Oak leaves, textured gold and bronze chrysanthemums and a simple modern ceramic container with orange and gold stripes make the brilliant autumnal color symphony.

VI. The still life is a composition of small household articles—fruit, bottles, flowers, books, and similar inanimate objects. Here a wine decanter and glass holding wine, a plate holding bread, a bottle filled with flowers and a napkin placed casually on the table imply activity and invite the participation of the viewer. Loosely grouped flowers are part of the theme, differentiating this still life from the arrangement with accessories, as in Plate 43, in which flowers are dominant.

or to put reaction into, a form recognizable by viewer or judge, if you do not identify yourself through knowledge and sympathetic understanding with your subject.

It is possible to suggest Mexico by using a sombreroed peon asleep beside a cactus but this trite figurine has been overworked to the point of banality. Actually, it is a very poor and unrealistic symbol for it does not take much imagination to realize that he would hardly be sleeping so peacefully were it a real cactus! Also, if you are interested in or sympathetic with the spirit of Mexico, this does not portray either the people or their customs. In Plate 70, native materials (yucca and pulque) and traditional national colors (red, green and omnipresent black) create a subtle suggestion of Mexico, reinforced by including the black pottery donkey bell from Oaxaca as an accessory.

5

Creativity and the Art of Observation

Flower arrangers have long been cautioned to develop a "seeing eye" in order not to overlook the tangible material things which nature supplies so abundantly: the tiny seed pods, the driftwood, the kaleidoscopic color in a mass of wild flowers. And these are all around us, to be observed and to guide our hands as we design with natural materials.

But it seems to me that the seeing eye is needed even more for the things that are *not there*. The spaces and voids and crevices left by nature in her own endlessly varied design plan. The wide carved spaces that can be seen in the indented aralia leaf. The asymmetrical voids that occur as sculptured plants rise from a rounded ground cover. The quietly restrained interstices of fern fronds in the half-light of the woodland. The jagged crevices in pine trees. The clean sweep of triangular nothingness as the clump of birch push out from a green carpet. These are the things that should invite your curiosity.

Principles of Design

Over the centuries, curiosity about the forces of nature has led man to an understanding of certain fundamental truths which we call the principles of design: balance, dominance, contrast, rhythm, proportion and scale. These are the principles which, consciously or otherwise, guide artists in all media of self-expression.

Balance is related to the law of gravity and to our own vertical axis. In all designing, any arrangement or composition, there is an imaginary vertical axis. All placements of material must reinforce the visual stability about this axis. In symmetrical balance (also known as formal and static), the axis is centered and the placements are equal on each side. Such balance, which is geometric and precise, recurs throughout history in the works of man, from the Parthenon in Greece to the crystal goblet on your dinner table. But perfect symmetry is a rarity in plant material because nature refuses to copy herself, even in two sides of the same blossom.

Asymmetrical balance is dynamic, informal, expressive and free, and plants adapt readily to it. Since the material on one side of the imaginary vertical axis is not equal to the material on the other side, some compensations must be made to achieve balance. All the attributes of the plant—size, shape, color, texture—and its space relationship to the axis are factors to be considered. Heavy textures, brilliant colors, filled spaces, strong shapes all weigh more than their opposites of neutral or grayed color, empty space, and indefinite shape. That is to say that one small bright geranium on one side of the imaginary axis will weigh more than lots of baby's breath on the other side. Space counts positively, that is, the greater the distance between the axis and the object, the heavier the object weighs visually.

How does the arranger know where the imaginary axis occurs? Generally all the major lines of the design intersect at the point through which the imaginary axis should be visualized. In traditional design this intersection is usually at the point where the axis rises from the container (center of weight). In free-style and abstract design, the visual axis is arbitrarily established by the arranger, with or without a container, in a preconceived volume of space. The lines

44. The basic intent here was to create an asymmetrical design of diagonal lines offset by curves. The magnificent blossom of *Philodendron Selloum*, velvety cream-white inside and sleek green outside, was the dominant flower with fresh green bamboo continuing the diagonal thrust. A controlled pattern of ti leaves creates an opposing diagonal line while the avocado and papaya supply needed weight and textural contrast in this polished mahogany leaf tray from Haiti.

and forms are balanced about this imaginary axis by the visual weight or force they exert as required to achieve the design purpose of the arranger.

I do not want to dismiss too lightly the subject of balance, but it seems to me important to mention that balance is instinctive. Even a very young child uses his outstretched hands to create a balancing factor when walking the crack of a sidewalk and the ability to achieve balance does not diminish as one grows older.

Dominance, also called the principle of unity, evolves from the natural law of survival of the fittest. To have dominance, subordination is needed, since there can be no winners without losers.

45. There is dominance here—of oblique line, of dark rather than light, of contour rather than plane. Interest is divided over several spheres of influence—around the spathiphyllum blossom and leaf at the right, the opposing diagonal at the apex, the knob by the branch at the left, and, in depth, at the inverted V formed in the crotch of the wood. Balance is asymmetric—side to side and front to back—and the off-center placement of the Chinese pewter cylinder on the weathered wood base is a factor in achieving visual stability.

In conventional design there was always a winner among the elements of texture, color, form and line. These winners, the strongest materials, were always placed dominantly at one point in the design. The "focal point" as a concept of floral art fell from grace when three-dimensional depth was added to the arranger's working vocabulary. Subsequently, arrangers spoke instead of "area or center of interest." Both phrases are now more or less obsolete.

Today, in free-style and abstract arrangements, the principle of dominance of elements at one point or area has been superseded by the recognition that there need not be a battleground, a contest of winners and losers among the materials. The materials and their strengths may be distributed anywhere that the arranger elects to do so. There is another change. The idea that *things* must dominate has given way to the idea that a feeling, an attitude—intangibles, in short —may dominate the work, with all parts of the design flowing into each other, relating to each other, backing each other up only for the purpose of allowing the artist a maximum of creativity and self-expressiveness.

Contrast as a word has been so well absorbed into our everyday vocabulary that it hardly needs explanation as a design principle. If there were no light, there could be no dark; there is no smooth without rough, no happy without sad. But everything is a matter of degree. Life as well as flower arrangement is softer, smoother, easier when the contrast is graded and easy. But as walking up a gentle slope of a country path compares with the excitement of mountain climbing, so the moderately contrasty design compares with the heavily contrasted one. Much of today's design has shock value which is based on contrast. Op art, for example, uses violent contrasts of line and color or value (since much of it is done in black and white) to create its characteristic quality.

Too much contrast is overpowering, too little is dull, but there should be some of each. In examining successful designs, you will

46. Again drawing on the resemblance which flower arrangement bears to sculpture (in both arts, forms and shapes are real and three-dimensional rather than illusionary, as they are in painting) one can relate this design to sculpture carved out of solid masses. Although there is linear emphasis achieved with pussy willows the dominance here is on mass; the technical term for such combinations is massed-line design. Textural relationships are fully explored with open-patterned philodendron leaves, shiny striated aspidistra leaves and contorted dried immature date palm.

47. Few trees have greater contrast within their own structure than the pine. In this contemporary free-style arrangement, a pine tree has been taken apart, analyzed and reassembled to exploit the dynamic contrasts. Swirling dry limbs form the basic line and space pattern. Fresh, new growth, stripped of its needles, adds contrasting straight line and texture. Opposing the stolid horizontal direction of the striated modern Japanese container, the bristly, radiating organization of pine needles is the nucleus of the arrangement.

find that the plants used often have one element in common and another in contrast. That is, if plants are sharply contrasted in size, they may be identical in color; if contrasty in texture, alike in size, etc. This is not a rule, but a useful bit of observation.

Think also of contrasts in shapes: dynamic with static or, a more interesting contrast, horizontal with vertical and recumbent, trailing or twining materials used for transition.

Examine and re-examine all good designs of every type to understand how and why they succeed.

Rhythm in design recognizes the cyclic quality of life, the recurring natural pattern in the days of the week, the months of the year, of season following season. We are scarcely aware of these rhythms, any more than we are aware of breathing, until a sudden interruption brings them sharply into focus, as would be the case if hiccups broke into the ordered pattern of our breathing.

It seems to me that rhythm is the most compelling of all the natural principles. I can conceive of living in the gray, neutral monotone of a world without contrast or dominance, but life without orderly cycles, and progressive beats and measures, would be chaotic, and chaos is the antithesis of order and design.

Contemporary art is absorbed with rhythm. In the past century there has been a new sound to music and a new choreography in dance, evolving from conventional cadence or rhythmic patterns but distinctively modern. Changes in flower arrangement have been more recent, occurring perhaps in the last decade. Even in the last few years the whole pattern of design in flower arrangement has changed, and the floral artist of another day would scarcely recognize today's forms. There are new kinds of units, new relationships between units, and a new type of grouping; the total result we call spatial organization. In conventional design the rhythmic pattern was clearly delineated by the line itself—crescent, Hogarth curve—while in modern design the viewer must participate in the completion of the movement suggested by the artist's distribution of interest points.

There is a dramatic contrast between the circular, lilting rhythms defined by the linear pattern in Plate 48 and the irregular, erratic beat of the spatial organization in Plate 31. In the former, the eye moves slowly up one line, glides across and swings rapidly down another, only to be caught up by an ascending line, much in the spirit of a carnival roller coaster. You cannot extricate yourself from the undulating and involved linear pattern. Very different in tempo, Plate 31 requires conscious and deliberate movement from point to point over an intricate, staccato movement—from shell ginger to angel wing begonia, from nodule to nodule on the locust branches.

Scale and proportion are principles involving size and interaction of units. Scale is the relationship of component parts; proportion is the relationship of those parts to the whole. Like the interior designer using

48. **Modern sculpture has been said to have several forms: designs carved out of masses, designs with mobile pieces, and designs of open, cagelike structures. This flower arrangement can be related to the last type. Emphatically linear, it is full of interlocking cages which enclose aerial volume in many shapes and rhythms. The lily blossom stems, contorted by a chemical spray weed killer, suggested an abstract drawing in space, a kind of three-dimensional doodling! Combined with a peeled, washed root that defines the primary space shape, the lilies add to and embellish it. The square gray and rectangular blue-green Chinese ceramic pillows on the modern stand made a strong, geometric structure that not only supports but also intensifies, through contrast, the organization of free-form space shapes.**

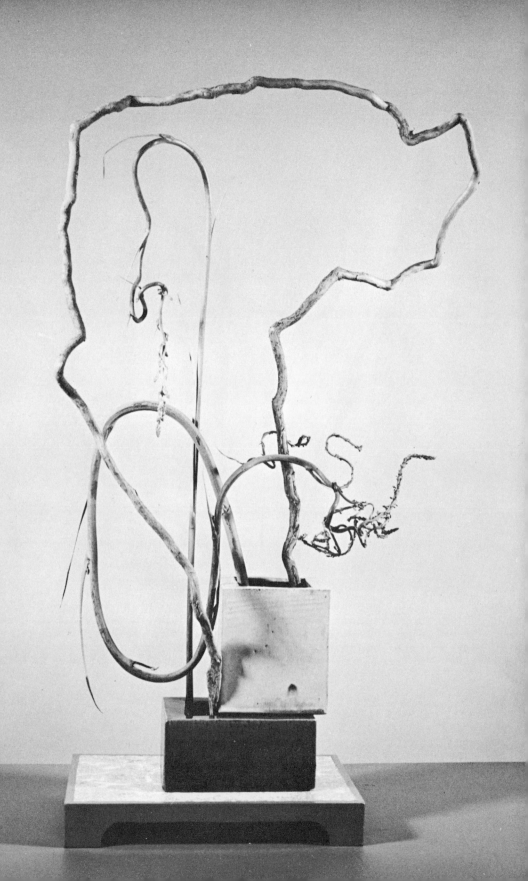

49. The better to display the excellent scale relationship of its parts and its unique stem line, a cluster of pandanus fruit from Florida was impaled on a sharpened one-quarter-inch dowel and set on a pinholder in the container. Anise stems, contorted by a chemical spray, were painted matte black to match the usubata. The design is noteworthy for well-proportioned voids, clearly delineated.

small furniture in a small room, the arranger can control size impression by using scale as a tool. She can make an orchid gross by juxtaposing it with gypsophila or weak by combining it with a large aralia leaf. Proportion, involving the size of units, is concerned with the size of the arrangement in relation to that of the container or of the whole to its setting.

The observant arranger can make many interesting judgments by keeping her seeing eye wide open and clear. For example, materials which are relatively poorly scaled to each other will look better suited if they are identical in color. Similar textures will make disparate materials seem more compatible, and backgrounds will seem to modify size, a black object looming larger than it is against white, a white object smaller against black.

I mentioned earlier in this chapter that rhythm seemed to me to be the most compelling principle in art, but the fact is, of course, that no one principle can stand alone. Each gains strength from the others, and all of them must be applied to the various elements. That is, there must be awareness of dominance, rhythm, scale, proportion and balance in the use of colors, sizes, textures, lines and voids in every design. I want to make clear, of course, that any of the elements can be used in an exaggerated amount—for instance, to create a mood of unreality, one might wish to work only in the family of misty blues, or only with grossly scaled materials to express absurdity. Each principle of design and each element will have its place in and its effect upon the finished plan.

50. Experimenting with the design potential of a direct light source, this six-foot-high arrangement uses the strong form of various kinds and parts of palm. The deep shadow has been handled as a vital part of the design area and included in the distribution of weight to achieve balance. Both form and texture extend into the shadow pattern to create interest and variety of silhouette. The dramatic contrast between dark shadow and the light palm flower increases its design significance to counter the dynamic horizontal thrust of the palm boot stem. Where a strong shadow is to be used, the arrangement should be constructed in place, for the direction and length of the shadow can alter the balance and visual stability of the composition.

Light

Light is "that which makes it possible to see," not a very profound statement, of course, but it is surprising how few arrangers have explored the dynamics of light. At every opportunity study the effect of light—the difference between objects seen in early morning sunlight or evening shade, how strong light flattens contours and diffused light enhances them. Shadows are darkest at the perimeter where they meet the contrast of bright light and longest in the winter when the sun is low in the sky. As everyone who has matched a swatch of fabric to a sample of paint knows, incandescent light changes color. Natural light is "white light" while electric light generally is yellow. It will intensify yellow or any color containing yellow (green-yellow to red-orange) but violet, blue-violet, blue and blue-green will be both dulled and altered by it. Green, like red, is only slightly affected by the yellow light. If you are doing a shadow box or niche, check the lighting before making your color plan. Some tube lights give a white light while others have a definite blue cast. The latter tends to dull the yellows, oranges and reds. If it is yellow incandescent light, be most careful in your selection of any blues and violets. Light affects materials and textures differently, too. A red rose that seems a perfect match for a silk brocade background fabric in daylight becomes darker and

These four photographs demonstrate the importance of lighting and camera angle.

51. (Left) In this example, a light from the left, above the middle of the arrangement, blots out details at right.

52. (Right) With the arrangement set close to the background, a single light from right front creates mood, but casts shadows which may obliterate the intended silhouette, as it does here. A more effective use of frontal light to strengthen the silhouette is shown in Plate 50.

53.   (Left) Two lights, one on each side and slightly above center provide strong contrast. But with the camera set just a bit higher than the table, the size of the container is exaggerated, its three-dimensional shape and other details are lost in shadows.

54.   (Right) Uniform lighting and a camera angle just below the top produce maximum clarity for this arrangement of dried aloe blossom stems and variegated leaves of *Philodendron verrucosum* in a modern Japanese container. The lights come from in front at both sides. Visualized in terms of a clock face, they are at 11 and 2 o'clock.

55. (Opposite) Why not a direct light source in the arrangement itself? Candles are self-contained but the possibility of fire must be considered. Contributing both fire-protection and color, free-form shapes of red-orange cathedral glass establish a strong structural design in the three-part ceramic container made by Ruth Holland. Red-orange glass float balls and crushed slag bring balance. As the candle burns, the flame will make a moving pattern through the glass, while the established rhythms of the bunching onions remain stable. Croton leaves add a new form and their veins pick up the color of the flame seen through the glass.

56. Mirrors reflect light and bring it into the design area but they also reflect the props! A two-inch hole in the upper mirror and a cup pinholder under it eliminated the need for visible mechanics. Twisted succulent stems and leaves of Boston fern create the line pattern, doubled by reflection. Distance from the mirror controls the apparent size and importance of a line or form. In the clusters of lavender chive blossoms, those close to the mirror become one form, doubled in size, while the highest cluster is shown as two forms, one real, one reflected.

57. Reading about Illusionary Art based on drug-induced hallucinations inspired this abstract composition. The idea is of seeing things in and out of focus, some appearing real and others imagined. Beginning with the organic form of a unique container by Tom Williams, lines and forms move in front of and behind the glass to achieve an illusory silhouette. There is an involved and overlapping rhythmic line pattern through which irises float upward. Half of a trimmed tropical palm frond adds texture and a free-form shape of crushed glass slag unifies the glass panel and the base plane.

duller under incandescent light, for it absorbs the light; the silk becomes lighter and brighter since it reflects the light. The planned relationship is lost!

Curiosity About Other Arts

Many arrangers deplore that flower arrangement is treated like a stepchild, instead of being accepted as a fine art. Although museums—which are, after all, the caretakers of all the world's art wealth—do seem to be more and more interested in having arrangements designed to fit heritage rooms, the prevailing view seems to be that flower arrangement is a secondary art at best. This, I fear, is the fault of the arranger. Too many refuse to progress with the world, to understand what is going on in the other arts. They go on working as they have always done, exhibiting little curiosity about the changing face of design, never attempting to apply new trends of other arts to flower arrangement. It is true, of course, that not all art currents, past or present, have application to floral art. But no arranger should refuse to accept the stimulus which can result from knowing more about other arts and crafts. Be curious. Attend art exhibits, craft shows, read about new trends, study the evolution of modern art. In this way, you will help flower arrangement to grow in acceptance and you will grow with it.

58. A non-objective pattern in "Op Art" style. The illusion of vibration
is created by the sharp contrast between the intensity of the orange- and
yellow-striped background and the highly textured, strongly shaped croton
and sansevieria leaves. Brilliant red peppers, in front of and behind the
translucent glass panel, add to the feeling of movement in depth.

59. This assemblage of fresh materials was done just for fun. Playing with
the forms and textures of parts and slices of fruits and vegetables, it
smacks a bit of "Pop" art and New Realism, with a little "Op" art mixed in!
The flowerpot and stem, made by trimming a strelitzia leaf, suggest infinite
ways for expanding the use of plant material. At a flower show, baskets of
materials could be made available so that spectators could create their own
plaques. (This one was constructed with pins, toothpicks and masking
tape on a vinyl-covered celotex panel.)

6

Personal Expression
and the Creativity Award

"A purple rosette with ribbons attached"—such a small symbol of victory, but how big an achievement it represents! For this is the prize that will be awarded the winner of the Creativity Award, following the rules for flower shows established by National Council of State Garden Clubs, Inc. One of three major awards for artistic design (the others being the Tricolor and the Award of Distinction) the Creativity Award is the only one that allows the arranger freedom in the selection and combination of materials, providing only that some fresh material be included. Since the award is not available in classes for Corsage, Miniature, Novice, Junior, Intermediate, Invitational, Niche, or Table, the question arises: what forms *does* it allow? And the answer is exciting! The new forms, the mobiles, stabiles, constructions, collages, and assemblages, as well as flower arrangements, are eligible for the Creativity Award.

Personal Expression

This new award requires that *personal expression* be one of the qualities in the scale of points. What is personal expression? We know that *expression* means representing, picturing, symbolizing, a showing of

60. The starting point for this structure was my memory of an awesome
fire. Burned beams which I had found at the site were sawn, one of them
at an angle to represent the collapsed roof. Plumes of smoke were repre-
sented by dried plume grass set in crevices in the wood. Bright red
anthuriums (kept fresh in water picks) made a flamelike shape.

I disagree with some of the modern abstract arrangers who feel it is
necessary to suppress all pictorial or photographic references in their
work. Representation is legitimate when one is trying to evoke a feeling
created by a scene.

61. A purely abstract arrangement features contrasted forms. There is a vertical made by a defoliated stem of azalea, recumbent or leaning form of clustered blossoms, prostrate, spiral and diagonal forms made with water-washed roots, and horizontals expressed with cupped fronds of Parlor palm. When there is so much drama in the forms, texture plays a secondary role.

feeling, of character, of ideas. It means giving objective expression to inner experience, that is, to personal experience.

So far, so good. But how does one express oneself without words? Now the going gets a bit rougher. Cezanne expressed self by creating a new concept of design. He changed traditional perspective so completely that art has never been the same, in fact, he laid the foundation for abstract art. He tilted his apples, he prolonged the line of a house, he added another stroke on the mountain and what he then had on canvas was a still life or landscape as Cezanne saw it, a personalized design organization within a two-dimensional frame of space.

Alexander Calder had another vision. He was absorbed with movement, repose, and the relationship between them. First he invented the mobile in which each part moves on its own, yet is part of the total design structure. Then he went on to another type of construction. He connected wooden shapes of all sizes with rods and with wiry lines leading from one to the other. That is, he immobilized his mobiles so that they evoked a sense of movement, without really moving. Finally he developed the stabile. His stabiles were metal sheets, often perforated, with separate parts that were welded together. The shapes were abstract, often whimsical, and negative space or voids played an important role in the total design. Thus he created a bridge between movement and repose, he expressed self, and in so doing, he invented new art forms.

It cannot be done the other way around. You cannot sit down at your work table and say, "I will create a new art form, or a new type of construction, or a new flower arrangement." First you must have something that you feel compelled to say, then you must find or originate the means and the materials for saying it. And then, if you are very creative, you will have said something new and different and personal.

All of this sounds intangible, but ideas *are* intangibles. Fortunately, however, there is a language of design in which symbols instead of words are used to communicate ideas. These symbols, universally recognized, are discussed in the following sections.

Elements of Design

Design elements are ingredients. They are line, form, texture, color and space which acquire expressive qualities through long psychological associations. The elements can be considered individually but they are inseparable and interactive. Every flower, every leaf, every piece of wood, has color, form, line, texture and occupies space, but in varying degrees.

Line defines the shapes and creates the skeleton of a composition. It has direction and kind which, together, give it expression. Each direction of line initiates a general response. The vertical line relates to columns and man standing erect. It indicates dignity, nobility and aspiration. The horizontal line, associated with earth and man at rest, evokes feelings of calm, solemnity and security. The diagonal or oblique line, like lightning, suggests precarious balance, dynamic action, danger, speed. The kind of line—thick, thin, curved, straight— adds significance to direction and helps us to relate it to ideas or feelings. Compare the graceful and elegant dignity of the vertical line in Plate 66 with the stolid, masculine wood in Plate 69 or the forceful and majestic mullein in Plate 26 to see how kind alters the expression of the same basic line direction.

Form has many meanings. I use it here to include contour, and to describe the boundary line of a design, as well as the shapes of voids and solids within the boundary. Arrangements are made up of forms within forms. The forms may be geometric, that is, outlined into squares, circles, triangles. Or they may be shaped into cubes, spheres and cones.

Not all forms are geometric, however. Some are free-form, as are

62. All the materials should have at least one element in common and another element in contrast. Note here the unifying factor of form between
the plants and the charred wood, the contrast in tonal value between the
wood and the darlingtonia, the contrast in texture and the unifying factor
of color between furry tendrils of tree fern, smooth container and rough
wood.

63. In the rubbish pile where a crew was repairing a chain-link fence I found this wire with its erratic pattern. Painted black and manipulated into the desired shape, it looked like one of the modern sculptures of space enclosed by a wirelike frame. Two types of palm trimmed into shapes suggestive of weapons or primitive art symbols were also painted dull black. Introducing texture and color variation, the shapes of feathery Mexican desert grass complete this free-style, space-oriented design depicting Africa.

billowing clouds changing shape on a breezy day. Or the forms may be the shapes of living, moving organisms seen under a microscope. All of these forms relate to something we see in nature.

As we see these forms in nature, we become experienced in judging their attributes. Mother's round breast is a happy, pleasant experience, so later, drawing on our memory bank, we say that circular forms are as satisfying, as endless, as mother-love. In such ways, the language of design has been created.

But I would like here to re-examine a few of the clichés and generalizations that seem to exist about the attributes of form. A smoothly rounded circle is indeed a maternal form, but the circle which is roughly described with a jagged outline, enclosing an irregular shape of space, is hard, strong and uncompromising. A triangle, too, can express many different feelings. A range of mountains set on a wide base will seem massive, solid, enduring. A steeply pointed shaft, as in the triangular foliage of the agave plant, is threatening, awe-inspiring. The scalene triangle of a classical Japanese flower arrangement takes on the qualities of heaven-man-earth, that is, it has all the attributes, depending on placement and supporting material.

Space, which I have mentioned under form, is a valuable design tool whose status has changed most dramatically in contemporary design. At one time, space referred only to the air around the design. Now shapes of space are a real and important unit of the design, not only of flower arrangement but of sculpture, as in the work of Henry Moore, and the lively arts such as theatre and dance.

Space occurs in nature in many different ways. It may consist of water, of open ground, of sky. It may consist of lacy spaces created by tree foliage, or of solid vertical space between trunks of trees in a natural grove. That is, space may be irregular, or it may be rigid, it may be free-form, or it may be architectural. Space may seem to have been carved out of a solid mass, or it may seem to have been created by the weaving of spidery threads through the air. Awareness of the uses of space is one of the most challenging aspects of creative flower design.

Color is a design element that makes the strongest and most direct emotional appeal. Through association, we relate certain colors to happy or unhappy times and we like or dislike them accordingly. Bright warm colors of earth and hot midday sun advance and stimulate; cool color of sky and sea recede and soothe. Dull grayed color can be mysterious and strange, like misty shapes seen under water. Or it can be depressing, like one's feeling of sadness and aloneness on a rainy day.

Nature uses color in many different ways. She mixes brilliant color kaleidoscopically. Patches of wildflowers growing helter-skelter have no apparent relationship but the effect is good—with so much haphazard color it forces awareness of the larger view. That is, repetition and rhythm exist in the overall landscape, not in the isolated segment. Then nature uses analogies—the vivid greens, yellows and yellow-greens of spring; the gold, bronze and rust of autumn; the dulled greens, silver and charcoal grays of winter. Nature describes not only season but also time and place with color. There are dull colors of rainy days and climates, brilliant hues of sunny days and places. All of these are evocative, and all may be used to fulfill a plan.

Texture, from the Latin word meaning *to weave,* refers to the interweaving of threads in a fabrication and is generally used to describe the quality of the surface structure. The description of texture is frequently in the vocabulary of touch or sight. We speak of smooth and fine, rough and coarse, shiny and sleek, dull or matte. As we touch these surfaces, we record our sensual reactions, we memorize them as if they were multiplication tables. Later, we refer back to our memory to "feel" the texture we see. Softness, elegance, formality, are expressed with velvety surfaces. Delicacy has a texture like a spider's web. Informality, masculinity, are expressed with roughly woven

64. Some forms seem to rest quietly in space and others seem to *invade* it. To create shapes that are interesting as well as meaningful, I used two New Zealand flax leaves to depict the sails in an interpretation of "Spring Breezes." The sails gave enough reality to the scene to stimulate the viewer's imagination. Thus he converts the modern Japanese container into a boat and the trail of broken windshield glass on the oval walnut base into the wake. Two white spathiphyllum blossoms and a single hosta leaf contribute variety of form to the dramatic silhouette.

65. (Opposite, left) Here is a line drawing in space made by a thin scraggly stem with a few leaves attached, but to me it symbolizes strength and tenacity for the physianthus vine, denied a structural support, looped back on itself in a desperate effort to survive. The Oaxaca black pottery hurricane lamp repeats the loop; the dramatic *Aechmea fasciata* bloom seems to be the source of the tendrils.

66. (Opposite, right) The decisiveness of the pattern, the verticality of the design, the use of only a few materials and the dominance of a light-reflecting surface add up to an expression of dignity and simplicity. The line begins in the pedestal of the classic alabaster compote and is carried through to the slender spathiphyllum leaves by the tightly organized swirl of deep wine-colored croton leaves. Bromeliad blossoms are in sharp contrast, in color as well as texture, to the sleek, lustrous foliages. To prevent damage to the surface of the alabaster, the arrangement is supported by a small cup pinholder painted to match the white container.

threads. The effect of texture varies under different conditions of light. A finely woven fabric, with light falling directly on it will appear harsh or sleek while indirect light will reveal the intricate surface texture. A highly textured surface in shadow will seem deep and soft where bright light makes it craggy and coarse. Here, too, we are able to build up material for our memory bank. In misty countries like England, texture is rich, soft, gentle. In sunny ones, like Spain, textures are sharply contrasted, hard and clear-cut.

Personal Expression and Abstract Design

In *Modern Abstract Flower Arrangement* Emma Hodkinson Cyphers discusses two major trends in modern design, abstract expressionism and non-objective abstract. In the former, she states, the artist is freely expressing a personal and subjective impression of an idea, feeling or mood. Non-objective, says Mrs. Cyphers, "begins and ends in the mind

67.   In this arrangement, the intent was to communicate the essence of the material. The material is a form, seemingly faunal in origin—a bird? a deer?—which moves poetically into space from many different directions. The forms are pointed; they grow one from another in a clearly discernible rhythm, each one facing a different direction. If you were to walk slowly around the sculptural design, you would have the feeling that *it* more than you was moving.

of its creator and has no subject, beyond the organization of lines, shapes, forms, and areas of color and texture."*

In view of these definitions, and the stress on personal expression in determining the Creativity Award, it is logical to question whether a non-objective abstract arrangement could or should be eligible.

First, it is necessary to inject some personal observations and conclusions. I do not feel that it is possible to achieve in flower arrangement, since the materials cannot be completely and unequivocably disassociated from meaning, the totality of abstraction that Mondrian was able to create with canvas and paint. Working with existing forms can never be as non-objective as inventing forms in their entirety. Second, in any form of non-objective art there are certain subjective manifestations. Being the work of one person it represents an individual concept of design relationships, which suggests some subjective and expressive commitment. Were this not true, ten arrangers given the same materials would create ten identical arrangements, but this is not the case. Each individual will organize the ingredients in a way that reflects her interpretation of their design contribution as her own knowledge and experience dictate. It is my feeling that both types of abstract arrangement should be eligible for the Creativity Award if they are truly original designs since, in reality, either is the unique and individual creation of the artist.

*P. 12 (New York: Hearthside Press, 1964).

68. (Opposite, left) To convey the spirit of ancient Greece I used a classical amphora, with a base and stand for added height and weight. The
balance is formal symmetry around a strong central axis. Contrasting of
rough and smooth, soft and prickly textures gives variety but there is a
stately rhythm which encourages the eye to move smoothly through the
design. Beige bearded wheat, tangerine carnations and various types of
green palm echo the colors in the painting on the vase.

69. (Opposite, right) Any designer working for personal expression must
utilize materials which have a strong and living personality. Forms like the
entwined aloe leaves are terrifyingly alive and threatening. One has the
feeling that the tentacles are capable of extending a fatal embrace—to the
driftwood column, or for that matter to us, if we foolishly got in their way!
The yucca leaves have a somewhat hostile quality, but are not nearly as
menacing as the aloe.

Judge with Creativity

After the blue ribbon winners in the eligible classes have been se-
lected, the time comes to evaluate them for the Creativity Award. The
award was designed to recognize an arranger's contribution to the
development of flower arrangement through original design and sincere personal expression. It is not intended to reward difference for
its own sake. To be worthy of her job, the judge must eliminate personal preferences. She must know the current trends in flower arrangement and other arts.

When all of the exhibits are traditional, the arranger who uses new
or unusual materials, dramatic color or dynamic line to forcefully
express her theme might receive the Creativity Award. However,
judging conventional design against contemporary free-style or abstract arrangement is entirely different. No matter how rare the material or compelling the color, the arrangement using traditional design
patterns is not as original as the free-style or abstract design that is
the unique creation of the artist. If of equal quality in application of
the principles of design and craftsmanship, the free-style or abstract

70. Interpreting the theme, Mexico, this work uses typical articles like the Oaxaca olla and donkey bell for their pictorial quality but it is color that underscores and validates the interpretation. Mexico is a land of intense color in violent contrasts, against omnipresent somber blacks and grayed earth tones. Brilliant green and red caladium leaves make a splash of color against the silvery dried pulque flower stalk with fresh green yucca leaves for transition. Three values of red in the grosgrain ribbon repeat the vertical line of pulque and lead to the black base.

arrangement should be given the Creativity Award. If all of the arrangements being considered are contemporary free-style or abstract, originality of design, significance of expression and degree of communication will decide the award.

It is difficult, but sometimes necessary, for a sincere and dedicated judge to withhold an award. Do not let kindness or outside pressure force you to recognize an exhibit that you do not feel is worthy. The Creativity Award will have real meaning and inspire exhibitors to new heights of design exploration and personal expression if the award is presented only when an arranger has made an outstanding contribution to the advancement of flower arrangement as an art.

7

Creativity—New Forms, New Words

The visitor at a flower show might well wonder if the term flower arrangement is relevant to the work being done today since in most contemporary shows everything from weathered wood to rusty iron is incorporated in the exhibits. Yes, indeed, there has been a change— in the form of flower arrangement as well as in its vocabulary. Exhibitor, judge and viewer have an obligation to themselves and to each other to understand the new language and the changing shapes it depicts. Here are some definitions of the old and the new in flower arrangement.

Conventional Designs

Conventional arrangements are classic, traditional ones. This includes the basic Oriental line arrangement, which follows the rigid rules established by the various schools, and the American floral designs—mass, massed-line and line arrangements.

Mass arrangements were originally bouquets, casual groupings of flowers displayed mainly for color and fragrance. Today's mass arrangements are no longer "casual." They are sophisticated designs

71. A decorative arrangement in the tradition of the European bouquet. Weight is centered in the hand-turned walnut compote, and the materials become lighter as they move toward the perimeter. There is no focal area as such, but rather a pleasing display of warm, glowing color and intricate, varied texture which keeps the eye moving in, out and over the whole surface of the arrangement. There is a harmony in the closely related colors, bronze, gold, pale green and brown, but sufficient contrast of form and texture to eliminate monotony.

with color and texture carefully controlled. Various geometric shapes are used symmetrically or asymmetrically: triangle, oval, circle, semicircle. A center of interest and an overall interlocking pattern are typical. The weight is generally centered at the focal area, where the vertical axis intersects the rim of the container. These arrangements are primarily decorative in purpose, particularly effective for churches, traditional homes, teas and banquets, where a pleasing design making a pretty picture is required.

Classical Japanese flower arrangement has had tremendous influence on American design. It introduced an open, linear design in an asymmetrical triangle that put emphasis on the natural growth and individuality of materials. It encourages arrangers to look to plant material for inspiration. From this interest in Japanese flower arrangement, the American *line arrangement* developed with its own patterns —vertical, horizontal, circular, Hogarth curve and triangular. In line arrangement, the design evolves from the material which creates the dominant line direction. Restraint is used in adding to it. The Western contribution is the addition of a focal area to replace the *nemoto* or trunk line of the classical Japanese flower arrangement. The emphasis, in line design, is on simplicity and a clearly defined, open silhouette. The line arrangement is not purely decorative, for in exert-

72. A modern mass arrangement which takes its cue from the old Oriental brass and cloisonné vase is a study of form, color and texture. The golden veins of the bird of paradise leaves repeat the color of the brass and seem to echo the incised design on the body of the container. There is a similarity between the geometric design at the top of the vase and the stamens of the artichoke blossoms. Generally asymmetrical, the outline is not rigid but rather an entwining, rhythmic movement of artichoke blossoms that lead the eye in uneven intervals and at varying tempo throughout the arrangement.

73. (Opposite) A vertical massed-line arrangement suggestive of autumn. Deep purple grapes and slender Japanese eggplants pick up the color and texture of the Chinese ceramic vase. Pale green immature Egyptian corn establishes the primary vertical line which is supported by the grouping of rough, green momordica, a vegetable called la-kwa by the Chinese. Distinctively corrugated dark green young palm leaves balance the organization of fresh okra.

74. (Right) A mass arrangement inspired by the antique French copper milk pail. Beaded heads of ripe Egyptian corn echo the texture of the hammer marks on its surface. The shaggy gold-tipped copper chrysanthemums carry its color up into the design. Florida palm boots, their stems protected by several coats of varnish, create the main structure and repeat the color of the polished walnut base. Contributing a strong color and texture contrast, the deep green, trimmed tropical fan palm leaves give substance to this five foot high arrangement.

ing personal preference in selecting dominant line material, the arranger can interpret a theme or express an idea.

Combining the color and texture of the mass arrangement with the
austere line design, the *massed-line arrangement* is exclusively American. All of the line patterns and their variations are used, but material is added to give them more intricate color and textural patterns.
The three-dimensional effect is increased by using additional material along, in front of and behind the basic line structure to give it
strength but not to confuse it. The massed-line arrangement can be
either decorative or interpretive and its added bulk makes it more
adaptable than the simplified line arrangement for the Western home.

Contemporary Design

Contemporary design, used to identify current trends in flower arrangement, is often applied specifically to free-style and abstract design. Conventional design has been abandoned by creative arrangers
as too limiting, and new design organization with more personal
identification with their medium, has replaced it.

Free-style refers to any arrangement that is not designed in one of
the traditional geometric patterns. It may or may not have a focal
area and the materials may be used in the normal growth pattern.
New and unusual materials, fresh, dried or treated, are used in combination with man-made materials. As arrangers became more and
more interested in creating original design, it was obvious that they
would have to manipulate or alter plant material, discarding traditional organization too. Interest was no longer centered in the focal
area but was dispersed over the whole three-dimensional volume of
space occupied by the arrangement. In *abstract* design, the arranger
uses the form, line, color and texture of materials as design units, to
express her concept of design organization or an idea or a mood.
There are two types of abstract design, expressive abstract and non-
objective abstract (see Chapter 6).

75. (Left) A line arrangement inspired by the graceful semicircular stem of green-gold cymbodiums. Three smooth, dark-green aspidistra leaves are in a strong dimensional organization reminiscent of traditional Japanese heaven-man-earth placement. The stem of the gold goblet continues the line of the orchids to the free-form redwood burl base.

76. (Right) A non-objective abstract arrangement has certain negative aspects—it should not evoke a real scene, in fact, no subject matter should be apparent. Its materials must seem unfamiliar and unnatural at least on first examination. It must not project a feeling that the artist has expressed an intensely personal experience.

There seems to be no universally understood boundary nor any specific criteria for distinguishing between free-style and abstract arrangement. Freedom from established patterns, stress on form and line, emphasis on total space utilization in three dimensions, is free-style or abstract in direct ratio to the degree of departure from nature and the amount of identification of the artist with the work through creative design and personal expression.

New Terms in Flower Arrangement

The inclusion in flower show schedules of many new forms other than flower arrangements necessitates a clarification of terms so that exhibitor and judge will understand what is intended. *The Handbook for Flower Shows* is the accepted reference for most flower shows and is well worth studying.

Still life

The still life is closely related to genre painting in that it takes everyday objects and groups them to tell a story or interpret a theme. In flower arrangement, plant material is included but only as part of the whole composition not to dominate it as in a "flower arrangement with accessories." The still life is based on normal relationships of objects and utilizes natural perspective which distinguishes it from the assemblage.

77. Expressive abstract design must be invested with an aura as real as the scent of flowers and no doubt just as invisible. In such an atmosphere, the gap between arrangement, artist and spectator will be a narrow one. Thus the spectator will become aware that the object is expressive of some concrete idea, feeling or mood.

My obsession here was to extol the growth forces of New Zealand flax, which shoots its flower stalk high into the air just before the development of its sharp, black satin seed pods.

Assemblages

There are three types of assemblage. In the first, unrelated items are used out of context as units in the composition to serve the design purpose of the arranger and in their new relationships to assume new identities. They may be in front of, hung from or attached to a background. In some areas this type of assemblage is called an *ensemble,* an equally apt description. The definition of ensemble as meaning all parts considered as a whole fits the Cubist-inspired assemblage in Color Plate II.

A second type of assemblage is the free-standing sculpture created out of one or more pieces of either natural or man-made material or in combinations of the two. To be eligible for consideration for the Creativity Award it must incorporate some fresh material.

The Pop Art composition, Plate 41, is an example of the third type of assemblage where units are organized in reference to a frame. The shapes of space are as carefully designed as the distribution of solids.

Other forms

New forms, grouped by *The Handbook for Flower Shows* under the heading of abstract arrangement are collages, mobiles, stabiles, as well as assemblages.

The mobile depends on the actual movement and changing relationships of forms in space. Mobiles are an intriguing mechanical prob-

78.   The mobile flower arrangement is one of the most fascinating forms of contemporary art. It moves through space and time (everything in motion does), a source of delight to all who see it. Piercing, spiraling, spidery, clawing shapes create a dynamic design that changes with the slightest air current, making it as difficult to photograph as it is delightful to watch. Here Australian Bull banksia leaves, Lobster Claw heliconia—whole and in sections—and pods of *Eucalyptus cornuta* are suspended from natural forms of weathered blue-gum bark.

lem for it is not only the shape and movement of forms but their actual weight that influences their distribution in the design.

The stabile, mentioned in the discussion of Alexander Calder in Chapter 6, is a ground-oriented structure that may or may not have moving parts. It is ground oriented through dependence upon supporting members but the organization of forms is *in* and *of* space— that is, it moves through and becomes identified with space by making incorporated and surrounding space shapes visible. To distinguish it from an arrangement that has a rhythmic design (a crescent or serpentine line), the stabile is an abstract organization of forms in space in an attitude of implied or impending or spent motion.

The collage could be interpreted as the first type of assemblage described above since it involves items attached to a background. Originally, the collage was used by the Cubist painters who put pieces of newsprint, cloth and advertisements on their paintings to embellish the picture plane. As a design form, it offers the creative arranger great latitude in choice of material and complete freedom of design. Organization of units is entirely at the discretion of the artist and can be expressive, whimsical, thematic or completely non-objective. Units

79. The structure, one form of the assemblage, is relatively new to the flower arranger. It is similar to contemporary sculpture except that the objects are found, rather than created. Natural or man-made materials can be used—driftwood, fresh-cut wood, parts of new or discarded machinery, rocks, shells, coral, or any combination that suits the designer's purpose— put together to evolve a form that occupies and includes space. Several pieces of driftwood from the same area that had weathered in the same manner are put together to make this structure to which two linear elements, grape vine, are added. The arrangement is displayed with a free-form base of water-washed gravel. Succulents and trimmed aralia leaves, kept fresh in plastic orchid picks, were added for color and form interest.

80. The collage is another form
of assemblage. This one uses
water-washed plywood found at
Folsom Lake as the background.
More pieces of plywood, some
with the laminations separated,
others in free-form shapes, were
applied with white glue to enrich the background for the iron
and wood pieces that create the
line and texture pattern. The
beautiful patina of orange rust
and sand on the various iron objects adds a striking color note,
while the touches of white in the
deeply indented wormy wood
give value contrast. There is
lively variation of form between
the irregular wood and the geometric man-made iron items.
Bits of kelp root weave through
the entire design. (Although
plant material, the kelp root
would not satisfy the require-
ment that fresh plant material be
included in arrangements under
consideration for the Creativity
Award.)

can be permanently attached with glue and nails as in the wall panel in Plate 80. As a temporary display with items pinned, taped or stapled, the collage can be equally effective and an excellent design exercise.

The Last Word

What is creativity? It is *you*. It is what you think and feel and believe, expressed through the medium of flower arrangement. Creativity comes from within the artist, a result of training, experience and insatiable curiosity about what is just over the horizon. The enemy of creativity is timidity. You cannot contribute to the art of flower arrangement without committing yourself to the search for original and creative design.

Bibliography

Canaday, John. *Mainstreams of Modern Art.* New York: Holt, Rinehart and Winston, 1965.

Conway, J. Gregory. *Encyclopedia of Flower Arrangement.* New York: Alfred A. Knopf, 1957.

Crowe, Sylvia. *Garden Design.* New York: Hearthside Press, 1959.

Cyphers, Emma Hodkinson. *Design and Depth in Flower Arrangement.* New York: Hearthside Press, 1958.

————. *Giving and Getting Awards for Flower Arrangement.* New York: Hearthside Press, 1956.

————. *Modern Abstract Flower Arrangements.* New York Hearthside Press, 1964.

————. *Modern Art in Flower Arrangement.* New York: Hearthside Press, 1959.

————. *Nature, Art and Flower Arrangement.* New York: Hearthside Press, 1963.

Derge, Wana. *Color, Form and Composition.* Berkeley, California: Wana Derge Art Association, 1966.

Handbook for Flower Shows, The. St. Louis, Missouri: National Council of State Garden Clubs, Inc., 1965.

Krauss, Helen K. *Shell Art.* New York: Hearthside Press, 1965.

Neumeyer, Alfred. *The Search for Meaning in Modern Art.* Englewood Cliffs, New Jersey: Prentice-Hall, 1964.

Reister, Dorothy. *Design for Flower Arrangers.* Princeton, New Jersey: D. Van Nostrand Co., 1959.

Rockwell, F. F. and Grayson, Esther. *The New Complete Book of Flower Arrangement.* Garden City, New York: Doubleday and Co., 1960.

Wilson, Clarice T. *Art Principles of Flower Arrangement.* Philadelphia: National Council Books, 1961.

Index